ENDOF

Many believers today have lost touch with the power of the anointing, and as a result, we're in danger of losing a generation. *Releasing the Anointing* by James Tan is more than a book—it's a clarion call to return to the foundational revelation of the Church and its divine purpose. Brother James guides readers back to the heart of the anointing, reminding us that it's not just a doctrine to be studied but a dynamic, living force to be embraced and released. Get ready for a transformative journey that will empower you to release the miraculous anointing in your life!

Alan DiDio
Host of *Encounter Today*
Pastor, The Encounter Charlotte

The anointing to grow, go, and govern. How simple but true is this statement which James Tan expands upon in this book. We have understood the grow and go, but as James points out, it is time for the church to understand that God's reign and government extends through the believer to the world around us. He has given us the anointing to govern!

Annette Capps
President of Capps Ministries
Tulsa, Oklahoma

I wholeheartedly endorse Dr. James Tan's powerful book, *Releasing the Anointing*. In this revelatory work, James masterfully navigates the depths of spiritual truths, breaking them down into practical applications that will resonate with every spiritually hungry reader. Divided into three powerful sections—"The Anointing to Grow," "The

Anointing to Go," and "The Anointing to Gather and Govern"—this book offers a blueprint for harnessing the divine enablement of the Spirit. One standout moment for me was when James wrote, "We are equipped in the anointing, not just to replicate God's works on the earth but to disarm the enemy as well." This profound statement encapsulates the essence of the anointing as a tool for both the miraculous and spiritual warfare. In a world that often feels overshadowed by darkness, we are called to release the anointing in greater measure, allowing us to work the works of heaven and assert our rightful authority in every circumstance. As we learn to shine as living lights reflecting God's glory, this book becomes an essential guide for anyone eager to deepen their spiritual impact in the world around them. As you read this book, I believe that you will receive deeply of these vital truths with a fresh impartation of God's power. Get your copy of *Releasing the Anointing* and discover how you can start releasing the anointing in your life today!

Joshua Mills
International Glory Ministries
Bestselling Author, *Moving in Glory Realms* and *The Miracle of the Oil*
www.joshuamills.com

Every Christian should read *Releasing the Anointing*. Dr. James Tan talks about all of the questions you have concerning the Holy Spirit and gives you the answers. He shares the importance of spending time studying the Word of God, praying in your language, and praying in the Holy Spirit, which helps to release the anointing. He shares about the different gifts in Romans 12, 1 Corinthians 14, and Ephesians 4 concerning the different anointings. Dr. Tan also explains the meaning of "baptized in fire."

I believe that every believer who reads this book and applies these principles to their life will be a blessing to their family, the Body of Christ, and an unbeliever.

Dr. Betty R. Price
Crenshaw Christian Center
Los Angeles, California

In *Releasing the Anointing*, Dr. James Tan takes the reader on a journey of education, impartation, and inspiration. In this book, you will discover the different ways the Holy Spirit wants the anointing to operate in your life. As you read through this book and apply its lessons, you will grow in understanding and learn how to practically yield to the anointing upon your life. I encourage you to read this book and go on this journey with Dr. Tan.

Kerrick Butler
Senior Pastor, Faith Christian Center
Mableton, Georgia

RELEASING THE ANOINTING

RELEASING THE ANOINTING

WALKING IN THE DYNAMIC FLOW OF THE HOLY SPIRIT'S POWER

JAMES TAN

Unless otherwise identified, Scripture quotations are taken from the New King James Version. Copyright © 1982 by Thomas Nelson, Inc. Used by permission. All rights reserved.

Scripture quotations marked NLT are taken from the Holy Bible, New Living Translation, copyright 1996, 2004, 2015. Used by permission of Tyndale House Publishers, Wheaton, Illinois 60189. All rights reserved.

All emphasis within Scripture quotations is the author's own.

Published by Harrison House Publishers
Shippensburg, PA 17257

ISBN 13 TP: 978-1-6675-0348-6
ISBN 13 eBook: 978-1-6675-0349-3

For Worldwide Distribution, Printed in the U.S.A.
1 2 3 4 5 6 7 8 / 29 28 27 26 25

For Bon and Boots.

And Kenei.

CONTENTS

FOREWORD

The Lord Jesus Christ made a stunning statement to His disciples shortly before His arrest and crucifixion. He told them that the Holy Spirit, who had been with them during His earthly ministry, would not only be with them but would take up residence in them. Jesus said it very clearly without stuttering, in John 14:17: "…the Spirit of truth, whom the world cannot receive, for it does not see Him, neither does it know Him. But you know Him, for He lives with you, and will be in you."

A tangible anointing is one of the major characteristics of the ministry of the Holy Spirit. It is the unmistakable result of the activity and operation of the Holy Spirit among us and within us. However, many believers would be hard-pressed to define it, much less understand its purpose in their lives. That is why I consider my friend Dr. James Tan's book *Releasing the Anointing* to be vital. He describes in detail the many and varied aspects of the anointing of the Holy Spirit, which enables, energizes, and encourages believers to fulfill their God-given assignments.

The anointing is not a feeling or emotion, nor is it optional. It is a divine imperative for every believer who possesses a heart to accomplish the will of God. Dr. Tan's timely and thorough examination of this essential subject will answer your questions and assist you in understanding the presence and purpose of the anointing in your life. Dr. Tan is a valued member of the City Harvest Network. His life and ministry have intersected with some of the most recognized names in ministry in this generation. He is uniquely positioned to describe and define the anointing, as well as how to benefit from it as we work together in the world's harvest fields in anticipation of the appearing of the Lord Jesus Christ.

Dr. Rod Parsley
General Overseer, City Harvest Network
Pastor and Founder, World Harvest Church

FOREWORD

Around 20 years ago, my son, Jim, recommended Dr. James Tan as an excellent guest minister at Living Word, the church that my wife and I founded in 1980. I invited Dr. Tan to come and speak.

As I watched him minister, I saw that God's hand was on him. He has a unique understanding of how to operate in the anointing of God and work together with the Holy Spirit to create an atmosphere in which God could move. He has a wonderful heart to serve God and minister to the Body of Christ. I invited him to come back over and over again!

At this point, Dr. Tan has been a longtime guest minister and true friend of our ministry. I've grown to know him over the years and have truly been blessed by his friendship and spiritual insights.

I'm excited that he has put much of what he has learned about the anointing of God into a book and made it available to you. This book will help you identify when the anointing is at work and show you practical ways in which you can access and operate in it. Dr. Tan also walks you through the Word of God and identifies the anointing working in familiar Bible stories and shows you what you can learn as a result.

If you've had trouble understanding the role of the Holy Spirit in your life or if you want to deepen your relationship with God, this book will help you. I believe the Body of Christ needs you to find and fulfill the calling God has placed on your life—and that will happen as you identify and understand the anointing at work in your life!

Mac Hammond
Senior Pastor, Living Word Christian Center

PREFACE

When God first spoke to me about writing *Releasing the Miraculous*, I also knew that there would be *this* book about the anointing.

I don't think you can ever have too much material to read and hear about the anointing. Nor do I think you could ever have a complete, comprehensive, *all*-inclusive teaching on *all* aspects of the anointing. This is simply because the anointing is, in essence, a current-day *now* manifestation of the Spirit Himself in the material earth realm. As such, there are infinite possibilities of how the Spirit can show Himself for, in, and through us.

As I sought the Lord on the direction I should take with this book, I sensed Him revealing to me an outline that I had known in part but had never pieced together. Isaiah 55:8-9 says:

> *"For My thoughts are not your thoughts, nor are your ways My ways," says the Lord. "For as the heavens are higher than the earth, so are My ways higher than your ways, and My thoughts than your thoughts."*

Nothing of God can be approached on the basis of academics *alone*. To presume this is possible would be to think that our human mind *alone* is capable of comprehending God. While we should train and educate our minds, both in natural and spiritual matters, the source of comprehending matters that pertain to God and the spirit realm must originate and flow from the Spirit of God Himself. This itself is a function of the Spirit and the anointing.

It takes the anointing to know the anointing.

It takes the Spirit to know the Spirit.

Not only do I believe and know in my spirit that there is a generation hungry for the anointing, I believe that both you and I have been drawn to study this so that we can increase in our spiritual sensitivity and efficiency!

SECTION 1

THE ANOINTING TO GROW

CHAPTER 1

ANOINTED TO KNOW THE ANOINTING

Anointed and Consecrated

While there are clear differences in the function of the Holy Spirit in the Old and New Testaments, there are also some similarities. In the Old Testament, the Spirit primarily descended on the prophet, the king, and the priest. Even then, the anointing in the Old Testament was only temporary and would lift once the task the person was anointed for was accomplished. Most significantly, the anointing in the Old Testament would only rest *on* individuals but not *in* them as it does in the New Testament. The saints in the Old Testament only had the sacrifice of animals to cover their sins. Under the New Covenant, we have the shed Blood of the Son of God Himself! The Blood of Jesus removes our Adamic sin nature, re-instituting our spiritual nature so that the Holy Spirit can dwell *in* us. This is why and how we are the *"temple of the Holy Spirit who is **in** you"* (1 Corinthians 6:19). We no longer have to visit a specific location to find the Presence of God as they did in the Old Testament; we now are carries of that same Presence! It is part of our "better covenant" (Hebrews 8:6) privileges to not just have access to the Spirit *on* us but to have the Spirit *in* us!

Once in my prayer time, through tongues and interpretation of tongues, the Spirit said it to me this way: "*The Blood cleansed you so the Spirit could fill you!*"

Since the Holy Spirit could not indwell the Old Testament saints, there was always the possibility that He be removed or lifted from them. Under this Old Covenant, when the psalmist prayed, "*Do not cast me away from Your presence, and **do not take Your Holy Spirit from me**"* (Psalm 51:11), he was praying a covenantally accurate prayer. The Holy Spirit could and many times did depart from individuals. However, in the New Testament, Paul, instructing the church in Corinth on how to deal with corruption and immorality among the believers, singled out a particular young man who was in a sexual relationship with his father's wife, his very own stepmother. Paul's apostolic counsel was that they expel him from their local gatherings and in doing so "*deliver such a one to Satan for the destruction of the flesh, **that his spirit may be saved** in the day of the Lord Jesus*" (1 Corinthians 5:5). This tells us that even in the depth of such sin, there was still the possibility of that young man being saved.

The Holy Spirit does not depart when there is sin, but His role in our life is diminished by ongoing, knowing sin because sin hardens our receptivity to the Spirit's voice in our life. We lose our ability to hear Him guide and teach us. As believers, if the Holy Spirit left us each time we sinned, how would we have the ability to hear Him call us back, to repent and overcome that sin? The Holy Spirit is faithful, even when we are not! It is when we fall that we need Him the most. The Holy Spirit is faithful, and He would not be faithful if He left us when we need Him the most! Obviously, as we see from the young Corinthian man, there is a high price to pay for choosing sin, and we should not take it lightly, but we must not forget that it takes the power of the Spirit to break the power of sin! The Spirit is always attempting to lead us toward depths of the anointing. Sin stops our ability to hear and obey Him; sin cuts us off that journey. The *Holy* Spirit empowers us to live *holy* lives!

The Holy Spirit is faithful, even when we are not!

Much of what happened in the Old Testament can also be seen as a prophetic picture of what the Spirit would do in the New Testament. Just as the only ones anointed in the Old Testament were the prophet, king, and priest, today the Body of Christ is comprised of prophesying sons and daughters and a royal or kingly priesthood (Acts 2:17; 1 Peter 2:9). Believers have access to the "prophet, king, and priest" anointing!

With each of these offices, the anointing didn't just empower them but it also consecrated them by marking them as separate to the Lord. They were called, singled out from the multitude, and were marked by the anointing as set aside ones.

Believers have access to the "prophet, king, and priest" anointing!

From *Vine's Complete Expository Dictionary*, we see that *church* (Matthew 16:18), from the Greek *ekklesia* (Strong's G1577), is a composite of *ek*, "out of," and *klēsis*, "a calling." So the Church are the called-out ones, separated from the rest of the world. The Church, those who have called on the name of the Lord and are born again of the Spirit, is a consecrated assembly separated to the Lord! It is the anointing of the Spirit that marks us and sets us apart from the rest of the world.

What the Spirit Helped Me See

It really takes the power of the Spirit to function in any aspect of our walk as believers. To be a disciple of Jesus is not a natural walk based solely on our natural desires and abilities. To be a disciple is a response to a call from God and requires the power of God to walk in and maintain. Peter realized Jesus was the Christ as a result of divine revelation. Despite the fact that they had spent time walking with and witnessing the ministry of Jesus, the disciples were instructed to *"tarry in the city of Jerusalem until you are endued with power from on high"* (Luke 24:49). Their walk with Jesus was not complete until they also encountered the Holy Spirit!

It takes the Word made flesh, Jesus (John 1:14), and the infilling of the Spirit to represent Jesus on earth! The Word and the Spirit are the two legs that believers stand on.

> *It takes the Word made flesh, Jesus (John 1:14), and the infilling of the Spirit to represent Jesus on earth! The Word and the Spirit are the two legs that believers stand on.*

We see three specific instances in scripture in which God bestowed giftings on believers. As I wrote in my previous book *Releasing the Miraculous*: "As believers, we belong to a gift-giving family! The gifts of the Father mentioned in Romans 12 are primarily for the strengthening of the local church. The gifts of Jesus mentioned in Ephesians are for the local church, the Body of Christ at large, and the world in general. The gifts of the Spirit mentioned in 1 Corinthians 12 are for both the local church and the world. The gifts in these three passages make up the earthly life and ministry of Jesus."

As God began dealing with me more about the anointing, He started to bring some amplification to my understanding of the gifts.

The gifts in Romans 12 are an anointing to *grow*.

The gifts in 1 Corinthians are an anointing to *go*.

The gifts in Ephesians are an anointing to gather and *govern*.

Any manifestation of God, through *any* category of the gifts, is always and only a result of a demonstration of the anointing.

The anointing allows us, in this natural realm, a peek into the multi-faceted nature of God. So, the anointing is God's way of reversing the wrongs of this fallen earth and bringing us back closer to His intentions for our life.

Answers to prayer are actually invariably because of an intervention from Heaven through the anointing.

God started showing me that there is an anointing available to believers to grow, go, and govern.

> *For I say, through the grace given to me, to everyone who is among you, not to think of himself more highly than he ought to think, but to think soberly, as God has dealt to each one a measure of faith. For as we have many members in one body, but all the members do not have the same function, so we, being many, are one body in Christ, and individually members of one another. Having then gifts differing according to the grace that is given to us, let us use them: if prophecy, let us prophesy in proportion to our faith; or ministry, let us use it in our ministering; he who teaches, in teaching; he who exhorts, in exhortation; he who gives, with liberality; he who leads, with diligence; he who shows mercy, with cheerfulness* (Romans 12:3-8).

There is an anointing available to believers to grow, go, and govern.

The seven gifts of the Father here are sometimes, and rightly so, called motivation gifts, serving gifts, or believer's gifts. They are so ingrained in a believer that they seem to manifest seamlessly through their personality. It's hard to tell where their personality ends and the gift starts. It almost seems the believer's nature to function that way regardless of the social setting they find themselves in.

Every believer is anointed with at least one and many times a few of these gifts. These are anointings that are dispersed throughout the Body of Christ. If you will study these seven gifts, you will find yourself among them!

For example, those with a leading gift will most probably be the ones who organize where to go for lunch after church. They'll also happily see to the seating arrangement at lunch! And they'll be doing that where they work as well!

Those with an exhortation gift will frequently have an uplifting word for those around them. They're natural encouragers! They don't need to "fast and pray" before they say anything that makes those around them feel lighter.

While all gifts from God are for us to serve others with, these seven gifts of the Father are truly entry-level, ministry of helps empowerments that the Body needs to function. Although these gifts are entry level, they are in no way insignificant. Local churches flourish when these gifts are in operation. These gifts see to practical needs, supernaturally. And equally important, these gifts flow through people and plug them in to serving.

> *Serving is the heart and beginning of all ministry! There is*
> *no ministry without a willingness to give to others!*

Serving is the heart and beginning of all ministry! There is no ministry without a willingness to give to others! The anointing is not for self-promotion but for self-sacrifice! The anointing enables us to give as God Himself would give. There is always an element of sacrifice in serving, but the anointing enables us to do so with a heavenly grace. *It is in serving that we develop and grow.* It is only in serving that we translate what we think we know from study, and desire to be of use to God, toward being an actual extension of God Himself. The anointing to serve is really an anointing to grow because serving is crucial for our growth and development. Just as the natural body cannot develop properly without some regular form of exercise, our spirit man cannot mature without a practical outlet to develop our spiritual muscles. Serving God is often expressed as serving those He sends us to.

There are no true leaders who are not also servants first! The Lord instructed me once, *"Don't serve and follow leaders who don't serve and follow leaders!"*

I sometimes come across believers who eagerly aspire to ministry, thinking of it only in terms preaching, teaching, or healing. They have romantic ideas of a public pulpit ministry but don't understand that that is only the tip of the iceberg! The heart of ministry is not to be seen but to serve! Serving might include being seen, but it might not!

The anointing enables us to give as God Himself would give.

Growing up Catholic, I had no aspirations or examples of being in ministry as I am now. I never imagined someone like me could teach or preach. My only concept of "ministry" growing up was to join a religious order and be a priest. That never appealed to me. After I got born again at 13 years old and started going to a Spirit-filled church, I found I had a great desire to help around church in any way I could. I didn't know much, but I sure was willing! I volunteered for everything from cleaning the bathrooms to working the guest speaker book tables. I often look back at those times and see that was really the beginning of what I do now. In a very real way, I still consider myself in the ministry of helps now. I may do it differently now—from volunteering at the church parking lot to teaching and preaching—but all of that is still basically serving people toward a path of growth in God. The anointing to serve is part of the anointing to grow!

He Anoints Us Where We Are

Another way that the Romans 12 anointing helps us is that it allows us to begin moving with the Spirit when we are new in the Lord and growing. No preaching or teaching ministry is born overnight. Moving in the 1 Corinthians 12 spiritual gifts take time to develop and grow into as well. But everyone can start serving in some way once they get born again. The Romans 12 serving anointing helps believers grow from convert to disciple.

In serving and learning to prefer others, we soften our hearts to move with the Holy Spirit. We can also learn the nudging of the Spirit as we minister practically among other believers.

Stephen, the first martyr of the Church, and Philip, the evangelist who had dramatic signs and wonders through his ministry, both started out as deacons serving the practical needs of the growing numbers (Acts 6:1-6). A *deacon* is simply one who serves. We have no prior record of any spiritual encounters that Stephen or Philip had. They had no previous prominence that we know of. Yet as they were faithful to serve, the Holy Spirit activated and matured the other ministerial anointing in them. Again, this is *not* to say that everyone should serve in the hopes of getting picked out for a position of bigger visibility. I am sure Stephen and Philip would have remained content as deacons had the Holy Spirit not moved them to something else. But it was as they served practically that they found their calling spiritually!

The anointing is yielded to in degrees. No one wakes up one morning a full-grown apostle or prophet—and I would be suspicious of anyone who claimed they did! We have to grow into the things of the Spirit. Growth requires time and experience. Just as no natural army would send a fresh, untrained recruit out to command a battalion of troops, God wouldn't send any of His children into the front lines of spiritual battles until they had sufficient training in cooperating with the Holy Spirit and working with the anointing. The Spirit wants to meet us and train us where we are! The Holy Spirit grows us by coming alongside us. He does not just call us upward but He lifts us upward!

The Sustaining Anointing

Studying the anointing should excite us for all the demonstrations of power that it will inadvertently produce. But none of those demonstrations through us would mean anything if our own personal lives were a mess and our lives or walk with God was cut short through the attacks of the enemy or a lack of wisdom. It is not those who start a race who get the prize but those who finish the race! We are in a spiritual race toward the call of God on our lives. It is not the intention of God to anoint us, move through us, and use us to bring deliverance to others, but then end up bound ourselves. It is possible to be so caught up in with the demonstrative operations of the anointing that we ignore the preservative aspects of it. God would not anoint us for mighty works to save others but then leave us to our devices to maintain our life and walk with Him. *It takes power to witness for Him, but it also takes power to walk with Him!*

I have found that the same anointing that enables me to minister to others will also allow the Spirit to minister to me. The same anointing that touches those I minister to can also heal *my* body and soothe my soul! Jesus didn't just open up the scriptures and heal the sick; He also fed the disciples natural food. When we prefer one aspect of the anointing over another, we miss the full spectrum of what God intends for us.

The anointing *on* us is to flow through us for others.

The anointing *in* us is to regulate our personal lives.

One is for ministry. The other is for longevity.

God doesn't intend for us to sacrifice one over the other. He intends that we have both longevity and ministry!

Like everything else about the Holy Spirit and the anointing, letting the Holy Spirit guide our personal lives takes intentionality to develop into. Public ministry for the Lord must be birthed and then sustained in private ministry to the Lord.

Many times, services in which I am ministering run long. I have led services that have gone almost six hours! It's not that I planned them that way, but as we gathered in hunger for Him and ministered, the Presence of God manifested so strongly that it almost seemed like chronological time lost its hold on us. On the other hand, I have had services in which we finished in under one hour and the Spirit still moved and ministered to many people. The issue isn't length or lack of time but the willingness to flow with the anointing in the room!

I remember one service in which about 400 teenagers sat, stood, or fell on their faces in quiet stillness before God. No one sang or talked. Even the praise and worship team fell out under the power of God! The quality of the healings and deliverances that took place from that one service astounded all of us. The testimonies started streaming in as some of the young people quietly went to the different leaders to testify about what God had done for them. We continued receiving reports of all that God had done for the remainder of that series of meetings.

Many times when I have hosted pastors' and ministers' conferences, I would preach sixteen times over a four-day period. When we had interpreters assisting me at these foreign conferences, we would need three to four interpreters to keep up with me! I normally did not have other guest ministers speaking at these meetings because this was usually the only time every few years that I would get with these pastors and ministers who had a relationship with me and allowed me a voice in their lives and ministries. I did have guest ministers assist me at other meetings.

During one of these conferences, one of the attending ministers noted my schedule and intensity of the services and asked me if I ever felt drained and depleted after ministering so much. I told him that I had truthfully never experienced being depleted or burnt out after ministering. I have been physically tired, but that is soon remedied. I told him that the key was that when I do minister, I share from the overflow, and only from the overflow, of my heart. I keep my heart full. Keeping my heart full preserves me. What overflows from my heart, I gladly share with others. If I emptied my heart each time I ministered, I'd put myself at risk of running empty. I give it my all each time I minister regardless of the size of the crowd, but I don't empty my heart. Ministers don't have to sacrifice themselves for those they minister to; they just need to point them to the One who did sacrifice Himself for them!

The bulk of my prayer and study time is not so that I can get a "word" to minister to others but for my *own* fellowship and walk with God to remain strong. *When we allow the anointing to be strong to us, we can afford for the anointing to be strong through us!*

I have been involved in the restoration process of a few ministers who had gotten derailed and fallen, some at the height of their ministries. Invariably, what I have noticed is that they derailed from their personal relationship with God and fell privately with Him before they ever derailed and fell publicly. They got skilled in flowing with the anointing in public to minister to others but did not allow that same anointing to minister to and sustain them privately. They had lost the joy of spending time with God on their own and for themselves. They had lost seeking Him to know Him. They had lost pursuing intimacy with Him. They were depleted privately but knew enough of the flow of the anointing to continue ministering publicly. This ultimately led to their lives and ministries being shipwrecked.

The anointing, because it is a manifestation of the character of God, is always seeking to bless people—even if it means speaking through Balaam's donkey (Numbers 22:21-39)! The manifestations of the Spirit (1 Corinthians 12:4-10) are *not* an indication of spiritual maturity but are *gifts* to bless others. As such, they are not earned but bestowed.

Gifts are given. Fruit is grown.

Gifts are given. Fruit is grown.

The Corinthian church had an abundance of spiritual manifestations but was also simultaneously riddled with moral and spiritual decay. It is a mistake to judge a person's walk with God by manifestations alone. Those manifestations could have come not because of the purity of the vessel through which the miraculous flowed but because God moved in mercy toward the faith and hunger of the congregation.

The remedy to balancing the outward anointing flowing through us to others and maintaining our personal walk with God is to *allow for the anointing to grow us and not just to grow in our use of the anointing.*

My ministry goal is to preach for an audience of One—God—and to preach to only one—myself! Just as Paul proclaimed that he spoke in tongues more than all the Corinthians (1 Corinthians 14:18), my personal goal is to always be the hungriest person for God in any room I am ministering in. Obviously this does not mean I don't have a heart for people or that I see myself as more important than them. It simply means that I recognize divine order. God works through *root before fruit!*

I have found that God wants to speak to me and not just through me.

If we follow Him, the Holy Spirit will lead us to intimacy before ministry!

Anointed to Behold

But we all, with unveiled face, beholding as in a mirror the glory of the Lord, are being transformed into the same image from glory to glory, just as by the Spirit of the Lord (2 Corinthians 3:18).

The anointing to grow is ever present because God is always wanting communication with us. Growth in God is an ever-unfolding revelation of who He is, and the only way to see Him is to have the Holy Spirit show Him to us.

The anointing to grow is an anointing to see Jesus because it is as we see Him that we become like Him. Many times this anointing to see Him will manifest as a stillness to hear Him (Psalm 46:10). Many times, this supernatural stillness comes in the room during corporate worship. *When such a still Presence comes in the room, reverence is the only appropriate response.* I have witnessed that oftentimes when this divine stillness comes in the room, those who haven't been used to this level of intimacy in their personal time get antsy. They'll start clapping, singing, or publicly giving a prophetic word just so they could be doing something instead of being face to face, as it were, with His Presence.

> **The anointing to grow is an anointing to see Jesus because it is as we see Him that we become like Him.**

All anointings require a response—and the only respectful response when you are in the Presence of the King is to simply, reverently, internally, if not externally, bow low and wait for the King to initiate.

Of course, there are times to clap, sing. and prophesy. But imagine if you were granted an audience with the Queen of England and, upon being presented to her, that's what you immediately started doing! Not only would that be disrespectful, but her security detail would swiftly usher you out of her presence! On other occasions, if the Queen were making a public appearance or speech, clapping and cheering would be the appropriate response. If we can understand that protocol for earthly royalty, how much more so do we need to learn protocol for being in the Presence of the King of kings?

A solemn Presence can also manifest in our personal prayer time when we are quietened, not asking or petitioning Him for anything. Many times when this happens I have personally experienced crying and shaking. Not just emotionally, but it seemed like my mortal being was reacting and responding to being in the Presence of divinity. Like it did when I have experienced it corporately, time seemed to be suspended. Also, as with the corporate encounter, I noted that I could walk away from that prayer time and still maintain a strong sense of that Presence for quite a few days afterward. I asked the Lord about this, and He spoke to me that His will was to "inhabit, not just visit"!

One the most precious lessons I have gleaned from these moments has been that I can turn my awareness of Him inward and develop an ongoing attuned-ness to the Presence of God. The Presence does not show up only when I am aware of it. His Presence is actually always in us as believers because we are the temple of God. But my acknowledgment of His being allows me the benefits of enjoying His company. The anointing always leads us back to Him because the anointing emanates from His being!

Being still before God is almost a lost art in some parts of the Body of Christ. It is in a place of quiet contemplation that many a deep working of the Spirit is established. George Fox founded Quakerism in the 17th century. Being still was one of the key components of their worship gatherings. Eastern Orthodox and Roman Catholic orders have also sought to practice silence and stillness as a form of spiritual discipline. But while being still *to seek* the Presence is not a new idea and is a worthy discipline to develop, being still *while in* the Presence is what transforms us into His image. Being in His Presence is being in the secret place where we are safe and embraced by the Father. I would explain it this way—if the Presence of God were a geographical location, the anointing would be the glorious climate of that terrain. When we experience the anointing tangibly, environmentally, we are literally in the Presence of God!

The Anointing Represents the Holy Spirit

> *It shall come to pass in that day that his burden will be taken away*
> *from your shoulder, and his yoke from your neck, and the yoke will*
> *be destroyed because of the **anointing oil*** (Isaiah 10:27).

All throughout scripture, we see that the anointing oil is a symbol for the Holy Spirit. So the strength and power of the anointing is in essence because it is the strength and power of the Holy Spirit Himself. *The anointing represents the Holy Spirit and the Holy Spirit manifests as the anointing.* For this reason, when I am teaching, as I will be in this book, the terms *anointing* and *the Holy Spirit* are used interchangeably. The Holy Spirit is the sole source of the anointing!

CHAPTER 2

A KNOWING ANOINTING

But you have an anointing from the Holy One, and you know all things

(1 John 2:20).

The anointing is not just for fuzzy warm feelings and goosebumps! While the anointing can touch our emotions, there are also very corporeal benefits that the anointing produces.

A major function of the anointing to grow us is that the anointing can guide and instruct us. Of course, as prophesied by Jesus, guidance and instruction are part of the ministry of the Holy Spirit toward the believer, which in turn is an amplification of the ministry of Jesus. So this function of the anointing is one of the branches of Jesus' ongoing ministry toward the believer.

Every four years, the Olympic Games are hosted in a different country. Almost 40 different types of sports are competed in by hundreds of athletes every time the Olympics are hosted, each with different levels of skill and experience. But all of those distinctively diverse demonstrations of athletics are showcased under the one banner of the Olympics. There is only one Olympics Games but many sports and many athletes. It's that same way with the anointing. There is only one Holy Spirit and really only one anointing but many diverse manifestations.

It helps me to see it that way because just as there is only one Jesus who offers us many benefits, there is also only one Holy Spirit who has multiple functions in the life of a believer. The Holy Spirit manifests in various ways. There are not really multiple spirits, like a spirit of joy, a spirit of healing, or a spirit of love. Those are all different functions of the same Spirit. It really does help our faith and flow in the Spirit when we recognize how the anointing is manifesting in a meeting. But we should not think that any one manifestation of the moment is better than or separate from the one anointing that emanates from the One Spirit. In that same way, there are not actually many different stand-alone anointings, like a healing anointing or a breakthrough anointing, but all are really various shades of the one anointing that flows from the One Spirit.

The anointing oil that God instructed Moses to concoct was used to anoint Tabernacle articles, priests, and later prophets and kings (Exodus 30:23-25). Other types of oil were sometimes used throughout scripture for anointing purposes, but there was never a specific oil for individualized, specific purposes. There was not a different anointing oil needed for prophet, king, or priest. Symbolizing the Holy Spirit, it was understood that the anointing oil, once applied by the command of God, would consecrate the individual and release in them the necessary divine enduements to fulfill the purposes of God. So the same anointing oil would endue a prophet to prophesy or a king to govern. It was the same oil, but it would produce different manifestations. There is one Holy Spirit, one anointing, but different manifestations.

Some ministers, because of the call and ministry giftings of God on them, will have certain anointings more frequently prevalent in function as they minister. Even with a call and giftings that accompany that call, ministers must get acquainted with their particular flow of anointing so they can get better skilled in cooperating with the Spirit. *We all need to learn to work with our allotted supply of heavenly oil!*

Work with Your Oil

*See, I have called by name Bezalel the son of Uri, the son of Hur, of the tribe of Judah. And I have filled him with the Spirit of God, in wisdom, in understanding, in knowledge, and **in all manner of workmanship, to design artistic works, to work in gold, in silver, in bronze, in cutting jewels for setting, in carving wood, and to work in all manner of workmanship.***

*And I, indeed I, have appointed with him Aholiab the son of Ahisamach, of the tribe of Dan; and **I have put wisdom in the hearts of all the gifted artisans**, that they may make all that I have commanded you* (Exodus 31:2-6).

Bezalel and Aholiab are not commonly known Bible characters. No Sunday school stories are told about them. They were neither prophet, king, nor priest. But they are important to our study on the anointing.

They were craftsmen. They worked with their hands. In today's vernacular you would say they were blue-collar workers who worked a 40-hour week at a 9 to 5 job. And yet they had the Spirit on them and were anointed to be artisans! While not any more precious than in the New Testament, the anointing under the Old Testament was comparatively limited in availability since only certain individuals had access to it. So if under the restrictive Old Covenant, craftsmen could have access to the anointing, then how much more in the New Covenant, when the Spirit is available to all believers, should we also have all manner of anointed blue-collar craftsmen?

The anointing is not just for what we commonly view as "ministry"—teaching, preaching, pulpit positions—but the anointing is available for believers in all walks of life!

The anointing of the Spirit is for the Body of Christ, and the Body of Christ is not just contained to a preaching pulpit ministry! The

Body of Christ is comprised of believers from all walks of life. *There is an anointing to cover every aspect of our life!*

We Have the Anointing Within

In 1 John 2:20, John tells us that this is an anointing that "you have," so this is not an anointing that is coming in our future but that we already possess. It is a boost to our faith when we realize that we already have access to aspects of the anointing within us. The anointing is not a far-off, distant possibility. For the believer, the anointing within is a present, indwelling reality!

This particular aspect of the anointing that John talked about is not as outwardly dramatic and demonstrative but is absolutely crucial to our growth and protection as believers. This function of the anointing is in fulfillment of Jesus' prophetic declaration in John 16:13 that "*when He, the Spirit of truth, has come, He will guide you into all truth.*"

While the anointing on and through a believer causes us to "do," this anointing within allows the believer to know. This is not to say that we know everything about everyone, because this is not an ability to know everyone's business nor is it a "gift of suspicions"! But as part of our Father's protection over us and His desire for us to be like Him, He gently offers us inner guidance through our spirit man to steer us away from wrong environments into right ones. This is also a part of God's apparatus to communicate with us—oftentimes, a still, quiet leading, like a nudge or a slight push in a certain direction. The anointing within us manifests as an inner guide so that we have an inner knowing of right from wrong. It guides us through a contrast of "yes or no," "red light or green light," and "peace or no peace" sensations.

We can all remember experiences like this. We got into situations that did not turn out as expected, only to realize afterward that before we got involved we had a sense, a witness, not to get involved. But we allowed ourselves to be convinced otherwise, either by those around us or by our own rational self. We had allowed ourselves to be talked out of obeying our inner witness. I have had numerous times in my own life when I have had to believe God to be brought out of situations I would have never gotten into had I obeyed my inner witness to begin with.

A Certain Slave Girl

We see a clear example of the inward witness in action in the ministry of Paul in Philippi, foremost city in that part of Macedonia (Acts 16:12). Paul had received a dramatic night vision calling him to Macedonia. This was at a time when this region had not yet had the Gospel preached to them. So Paul had been sent there by the call of God to pioneer a work.

> *Now it happened, as we went to prayer, that a certain slave girl possessed with a spirit of divination met us, who brought her masters much profit by fortune-telling. This girl followed Paul and us, and cried out, saying, "These men are the servants of the Most High God, who proclaim to us the way of salvation." And this she did for many days.*
>
> *But Paul, greatly annoyed, turned and said to the spirit, "I command you in the name of Jesus Christ to come out of her." And he came out that very hour* (Acts 16:16–18).

This particular fortune-telling slave girl was a bit of a local celebrity. She had enough of a local following that it brought in financial profit for her masters. Actually, she was a slave on two counts. First, as was widespread in the culture then, she was evidently subject to a certain level of servanthood to her masters. Second, she was also enslaved by "a spirit of divination"—in Greek, *python* (Strong's G4436). In Greek mythology, this python spirit was a serpent or dragon that dwelt in that region and was said to have guarded the oracle of Delphi. It was by all accounts a demonic spirit, and it possessed this young girl—literally, "to hold," the Greek word *echo* (Strong's G2192). So she was held captive by a python spirit of divination. All forms of necromancy, soothsaying, and fortune telling are demonically inspired—tarot card readings, astrology, spirit boards, and the like. Like a python, they enslave by strangling and suffocating. Anytime anyone attempts to venture into the spirit realm without the aid and leadership of the Holy Spirit, it is witchcraft. Witchcraft is willing enslavement to demonic spirits. It is *only* the anointing of the Spirit that can destroy and break such dark bondage!

> *Anytime anyone attempts to venture into the spirit realm without the aid and leadership of the Holy Spirit it is witchcraft.*

Since Paul and the Gospel were new in this region, not many knew of him or the message he was there to proclaim. This slave girl latched on to the Paul and the ministry team and started attempting to walk with them. Interestingly, she was actually among the first in that region to recognize Paul and the message he proclaimed. Her proclamation that *"These men are the servants of the Most High God, who proclaim to us the way of salvation"* was accurate. Yet it wasn't the girl herself who recognized the validity of the Gospel but the python spirit within her.

James 2:19 tells us that *"even the demons believe."* Demons are not blind to nor are they unbelieving of the Gospel and the power of God. Yet they are still, and always will be, in decisive rebellion and warfare against God and His people. The question should be asked: why then did the demons, through the slave girl, seem to promote Paul and the Gospel? I have found when demons realize they cannot stop the spreading of the Gospel, they will gladly attempt to infiltrate the Church so they can dilute the message and exert influence over its direction. Undoubtedly, the python spirit's goal was that the slave girl be afforded some sort of eldership position among the blossoming work in that region. I believe that a man without the depth of relationship with the Holy Spirit that Paul had would have appointed the slave girl an elder or deacon at church! The benefits were tempting—she was more established, having been there longer, better known then Paul, and had a large enough following to bring in financial support. All desirable considerations in launching any new ministry!

But a red light—no peace, stop, anointed annoyance—arose in Paul. The anointing on the inside can warn and guide even when people around us are saying *all* the right things. They may look right, sound right, even smell right, but if there is no peace on the inside, then they are *not* right for you! Not having peace about someone doesn't immediately mean that they are demon-possessed, but it does mean that you should not proceed.

The slave girl rattled off all the right things but the anointing alerted Paul that it was coming from the wrong source! We can examine a person's fruit, but it is only the Holy Spirit who can show us their root!

Also, we need to make sure that we do not over-spiritualize our personal likes or dislikes of people, calling it "the anointing warning us" or saying they have demons. The anointing does not make you unsociably suspicious! It's only natural that there will be some people whom we gravitate toward personality-wise. Paul did not immediately act on his annoyance with the slave girl. Luke, the author of Acts and part of Paul's traveling team, records that "*this she did for **many days**.*" Paul kept silent despite his annoyance until he had clear direction from the Lord. *It is wisdom not to overreact to what the anointing shows you.* Tellingly, Paul did not go on an investigative hunt to see what was wrong with her or to see what demons she had. He simply waited till he was moved and instructed by the same anointing that caused his annoyance with her in the first place. He sought no other external confirmations. *Peace or a lack of peace is all the primary confirmation we need.*

When he was finally released by the Spirit to address the issue, Paul "*turned and said to the spirit.*" Paul did not speak to the girl but to the evil force of demonic influence behind the girl. The anointing will lead us with specificity to root causes without guessing or an elaborate witch hunt.

The anointing within, imparted to guide and grow believers, will lead us into the ways of truth, both in the things of God and in natural, practical, everyday issues of life.

A Little Bit About Demons

This passage regarding Paul and the girl possessed with a python spirit shows us clearly that the Word of God makes no excuses for the activity of demons. Neither does the Word of God apologize for the need for believers to confront and expel demons whenever necessary.

The role of the anointing is that "*the yoke will be destroyed because of the anointing*" (Isaiah 10:27). While it is true that some yokes are self-imposed, either in willful accord with demons or out of ignorance, the primary yokes that need to be destroyed are directly demonically initiated and maintained. Regardless of how someone gets fastened with a binding yoke, the instrument of deliverance and freedom remains the same—the anointing of the Spirit!

We should be reminded, as believers, that God made man spirit, soul, and body (1 Thessalonians 5:21). When a person receives Jesus as Lord, they instantly get born again, and they become the temple of the Holy Spirit (1 Corinthians 6:19), meaning that the Spirit of God dwells in them. The soul part of man consists of their will, emotions, intellect, memories, and imagination. This is the part of man that Romans 12:2 tells us, *"Do not be conformed to this world, but be transformed by the **renewing of your mind**, that you may prove what is that good and acceptable and perfect will of God."* In Romans, Paul was writing to believers, yet they needed to have their minds renewed to know God's good, acceptable, and perfect will. The body of man is the most easily recognizable part of man and the most changeable and subservient to the dictates of the soul and spirit parts of man.

Since the Holy Spirit Himself dwells in a believer, it would be impossible to be a born-again believer and be possessed by demons in the truest sense of having a demon occupy or own their spirits. The Holy Spirit lives in the spirits of believers and He will not share that space with a demon! So you could not be a believer and be possessed by demons in the traditionally understood sense of demon possession. I think the term *possessed*, as used in the King James Version and in some modern versions, leaves the readers with an idea of implied ownership, but that would be incorrect by translation and by theology. In the dozen or so times in the New Testament that the Greek verb *daimonizo* is used, it would be better understood as being *subjected to demonic influence* and not owned by demons.

Can a believer be demon-possessed—have their spirit owned and indwelt by demons? Decidedly, no! How can the Holy Spirit be made party to being a "housemate" with a demon?

Can a believer be subject to demonic influence, either in their mind or their body? Yes. But only with their allowance, either by ignorance or by deception.

What do they need in order to get free? The anointing gets them out from under that yoke and then maintains that freedom by renewing their mind to maintain a Word-filled, Spirit-filled life!

Too much has been made of "deliverance ministry." Alone, it's a fruitless endeavor unless it also, with equal intensity, emphasizes a need to put on the new man by the renewing of the mind.

Expelling demons is a function of the anointing *upon*, but that has to be coupled with the anointing *within* to teach, guide, and grow to maintain freedom.

Two-Fold Guidance

However, when He, the Spirit of truth, has come, He will guide you into all truth; for He will not speak on His own authority, but whatever He hears He will speak; and He will tell you things to come (John 16:13).

The guidance of the Holy Spirit through the anointing within can be said to have a two-fold direction. First, the anointing within guides us toward current truth. This would be present or past happenings and situations. This was the case with Paul and the girl with the python spirit. It was a few days later before the discerning of spirits revealed that Paul was to address a spirit (1 Corinthians 12:10), but even before that Paul already had a knowing that there was something about this girl that was not right.

Second, the anointing alerts us toward future events. Paul experienced this on his voyage to Rome in Acts 27:10: *"Men, **I perceive** that this voyage will end with disaster and much loss, not only of the cargo and ship, but also our lives."*

Like the previous encounter with the fortune-telling girl, there was no dramatic vision or angelic visitation. All Paul had was a simple

"I perceive." The anointing within does not guide loudly, but it does guide clearly!

> *The anointing within does not guide loudly, but it does guide clearly!*

In the instance with the girl with the python spirit, Paul was alerted by the Spirit to protect his apostolic mission and to keep the infant church pure from demonic influence. On his journey to Rome, Paul was made aware that the journey would end in ship-wreck even though, as a prisoner, he had no control over the trip. Part of the reason why the upcoming shipwreck was revealed to Paul, I believe, was so that he would have peace through the storm. God can show us of things to come so there is no uncertainty in our lives. Paul was not instructed to take authority over the storm or to pray. He was simply told that he would survive the trip. What Paul perceived in his spirit by the anointing prepared him for what was to come and steadied him that God would be with him through the storm. This aspect of the anointing assures us that God is here in our now but that He has also been in our future—and He is good enough to let us know that all is well!

I like theme parks, particularly roller-coaster rides. I always try to visit a theme park whenever I can. When my sons were small, I would try to bring them along with me whenever I could. Many times, because they were still little, I would go on the rides alone first so that when they got on it, I would already know where the dips, twists, and turns were and I could steady them as we rode through it. God wants to do the same for us! He has been to our future and wants us to know that He will ride with us through it!

As with the girl with the python spirit, Paul's initial, still, inward guidance was later amplified with a louder, more dramatic leading. In

Acts 27:23, regarding his trip to Rome, Paul recounts that "*there stood by me this night an angel of the God to whom I belong and whom I serve.*" So the "loud" guidance only followed the inward, quieter guidance.

> *I have found that many times the inner guidance of the anointing positions me for the outer guidance of the Spirit.*

I have found that many times the inner guidance of the anointing positions me for the outer guidance of the Spirit. When we take the smaller steps of yielding to the anointing within, of following the "peace or no peace" leadings, we move toward the place where more specific directions from God may be necessary and made available by the Spirit. Like everything else with the things of God, it takes faith to follow the guidance of the Spirit. Faith starts with small steps before it leaps! *The inward witness is an opportunity to be daily in the school of the Spirit in learning to respond to Him in faith and obedience. Following the "small" leadings is a way to practice being in daily, regular communication with the Spirit of God in quiet communion.*

The more dramatic leadings of the Spirit are not more important than the quieter leadings. They are usually not as frequent and rightly so. It is not the plan of God that His sons and daughters be *primarily* led outwardly. The Spirit dwells on the inside of us, so why would God's primary communication with us originate from outside us? To be sure, angelic visitations, dreams, visions, and prophecies are all scripturally valid forms of divine communication. Although we are biblically promised guidance and communication from and with God, we are not promised the vehicle of that communication. However, we are told that "*The spirit of a man is the lamp of the Lord*" (Proverbs 20:27). So we see that our own spirit, where the Holy Spirit dwells, is God's "lamp" that He uses to shed light from! He guides from the inside!

The anointing within is what lights our spirit lamp!

Needed by the Spirit

*But He **needed** to go through Samaria* (John 4:4).

The anointing within guides us *away* from harm but also *toward* the purpose of God for us. You could also say that the anointing within guides us away from situations that take away from our purpose and toward situations that receptively require the anointing we carry.

A major purpose of the anointing is to destroy the works of the enemy. So the anointing will always guide us away from positions that drain the flow of the anointing in our lives and in the direction where our anointing will flourish and overflow.

So we should stay away from people and places where we sense a red light, no go, no peace, and we should gravitate toward people and places where we seem to have a pull to a "deep calling to deep" experience.

In John 4, we see the anointing guiding Jesus strongly toward Samaria. This was outside of the social norms of the day for the Jews. The Samaritans insisted they were the true Israel and had their own temple on Mount Gerizim. The tension between the Jews and the Samaritans was so heated that some Bible commentaries record rabbis as saying that eating bread with Samaritans was like eating swine's flesh!

Yet the anointing within moved Jesus so that He *needed* to go through Samaria. The anointing can guide us toward places that seem unlikely but are hungry for a touch from God. The leading of the anointing is an indispensably powerful ministry tool!

Despite His disciples' shock and quiet disgust, Jesus decided to make an unexpected detour. Following the guidance of the Spirit caused Jesus to cross social and political boundaries in order to be a vessel of good news and deliverance. I firmly believe this is still true today. I believe that God, in His mercy, has called individuals in the Body of Christ to be messengers of the anointing and represent

Him to people groups and social spheres across a wide spectrum that would normally not be reached by pulpits on a Sunday morning. I believe there are leadings and anointings for the structures that form society. Believers must be led by the anointing into these spheres and be established there by the anointing so the King and the Kingdom can have necessary representation!

The anointing guided Jesus, not only to an unlikely location but also to an unlikely person. Whenever I study this, I am always in awe how the mercy of God knows how to find the spiritually hungry in the unlikeliest of places!

Meeting a female outcast at a well around noontime, Jesus talked to her and, by a word of knowledge (1 Corinthians 12:8), told her things that He could not have known otherwise. The guidance of the Spirit positioned Jesus to speak words by the Spirit and the result was that "*many of the Samaritans of that city believed in Him because of the word of the woman who testified, 'He told me all that I ever did'*" (John 4:39). The bonus miracle to this encounter was that the adulteress, the women at the well shunned by society, found a new role in life as she became an evangelist to her village, leading many to the Messiah!

The Everyday Guide

> *Nevertheless I tell you the truth. It is to your advantage that I go away; for if I do not go away, the Helper will not come to you; but if I depart, I will send Him to you* (John 16:7).

Many times when I read this passage, I ponder how Jesus' statement here must have perplexed the disciples. They had left all to follow Jesus, to the scorn and bewilderment of many close to them. They had seen and heard all they needed to see and hear to convince them that the long-awaited Messiah had finally arrived. Anticipation was at an all-time high for what they expected would be the initiation of the Messiah's reign. Then in the middle of it all, Jesus told them it was really to their advantage that He depart. Remember that there was little knowledge and revelation on the Holy Spirit in the Old Testament for the disciples to draw from. They had not considered they needed any Helper other than Jesus Himself!

Since Jesus said it was an advantage that He leave and the Spirit come, that would mean that we are not worse off without Jesus physically being here but rather better off.

One of the ways we are better off is that we wouldn't just have God *with* us but we would have God *in* us. For the believer, the guidance and protection offered from being with Jesus now includes having that same guidance and protection even while they were not in His physical presence. Really, having the Holy Spirit *in* us is a depth of relationship with God that the early disciples did not enjoy.

The guidance of the Spirit is vital to the life of a believer—not just in practical, everyday matters but in spiritual growth and developing an ongoing, deepening relationship with God through the Holy Spirit. It is fanciful presumption to assume that in our own strength we can walk the way of a believer. It takes a supernatural strength to live a supernatural life, and that's exactly what it means to be a believer.

CHAPTER 3

THE ANOINTING TEACHES US

Part of our growth in anointing requires that we have a grounding in the things of God. Primarily this means we need a workable, knowledgeable, living, breathing relationship with the written Word of God and ongoing intimacy with the Holy Spirit. Of course, there are many other elements involved, but any and all of those will basically be covered under both these headings.

The Holy Spirit, as the Representative of the Godhead on the earth today, is ideally appointed to teach us the things of God. The way He speaks, guides, and teaches us is through the anointing in and on us.

The anointing *in* us guides and teaches.

The anointing *on* us energizes and empowers.

Through tongues and interpretation, the Spirit taught it to me this way:

Divine direction comes from the anointing within us.

Divine demonstrations come from the anointing upon us.

We need both functions of the anointing, in and on us, to function fully as Spirit-led disciples. If we only operate with the anointing in us, then we will not be able to fully represent the dynamic power of God. And if we only operated with the anointing on us, then we will lack and fail in our personal lives.

Guidance keeps us safe and gets us to the right places with the right people. Teaching establishes and expands our walk with God. We need both the guiding and teaching aspects of the anointing in us.

The Helper Teaches

> But the Helper, the Holy Spirit, whom the Father will send in My name, He will teach you all things, and bring to your remembrance all things that I said to you (John 14:26).

Spirit-filled, Spirit-led teaching is part of the divine help we receive from heaven!

When we understand that teaching is one of the Holy Spirit's undertakings, it shows us not only how seriously God views teaching—so much that He wants to be personally involved—but also how much we would lack in receiving from Him if we ignore the Spirit's teaching ministry toward us.

The Holy Spirit teaching us is part of how the Helper helps us!

How the Anointing Teaches Us

There four basic ways that the anointing teaches us:

- First, the anointing brings and inspires to our remembrance the things that are in the Word.
- Second, the anointing can illuminate and expound things as we read, hear, and study.
- Third, the anointing teaches us through the five-fold ministry—men and women who are raised up in the Body of Christ.
- Last, the anointing teaches us directly by revelation—speaking and communicating with us.

Inspired to Remember

This manifestation of the anointing teaches us in two ways. First, it reminds us directly as we have need of things that have been said and promised to us by God. Then, this "reminding" anointing also functions as ministers are teaching and the Holy Spirit gives them inspired recall of points and scripture that they need to minister to people.

In some ways, Peter was the least likely to be chosen to speak after the outpouring on the day of Pentecost. For one thing, he had just recently returned to the Lord after he denied Jesus thrice. Although he had been fully restored by Jesus, it still took a level of love and unity for the other disciples to willingly recognize that the Spirit had chosen Peter to deliver the first address of the post-outpouring Church. From Acts 2:14, we see that Peter got up to speak *"standing up with the eleven."* So Peter may have been the one speaking, but he had the full public support of the others.

What a great picture of how the corporate anointing works. There was a supernatural unity among them. There was no pulpit political jousting for position, no suspicious side eyes, there was a unity of and unity in the Spirit! *Unity is a work of the Spirit that will allow a move of the Spirit!* The anointing leaks out through cracks of disunity.

Since this move of the Spirit was a "suddenly," no one was ready for or expecting what happened. There was no time to prepare notes for the message that was immediately delivered to the masses. Yet Peter instantly and seamlessly started the message by quoting the exact and relevant passage from Joel! Peter not only quoted Joel, but he had supernatural insight as to the meaning and fulfillment of the text and the spiritual implications! Another reason why this was supernatural was that Peter's background was in industrial fishing; he was not a scholar or professional student of the Old Testament.

Peter's flagship message on Pentecost is an example of how the anointing brings to our remembrance and teaches us. The anointing can affect our intellectual memory functions as well as give us supernatural insight to what He brings us.

Just like the Church's first message was preached by divine inspiration, so also the Church's first official martyr, Stephen, seemingly had a reputation for speaking by inspiration of the anointing. Acts 6:10 tells us that his detractors *"were not able to resist the wisdom and the Spirit by which he spoke."* Since it was both the wisdom and the Spirit that they could not resist, we know that Stephen wasn't just a good oratory debater. There was an unction on what he said that confronted those who opposed him.

So in both the ministry of Peter and Stephen, we see there was a flow of inspired speaking, complete with scripture quotations and cross references. There was even divine commentary and exposition on the scriptures quoted!

In Matthew 10:19-20, Jesus had promised the disciples *"For it will **be given to you** in that hour what you should speak; for it is not you who speak, but **the Spirit of your Father who speaks in you**."* So filling our thoughts and words with matters that pertain to the things of God and supplying us with inspired thoughts and utterances is part of the promise of Jesus to His disciples.

To be clear, study, preparation, notes, outlines, and references are all good, right, and acceptable for sermon preparedness and self-study, but equally as right and good is to make room for inspired teaching and preaching delivered on the spur of a Spirit moment. Additionally, the more one studies and prepares in private, the more the Spirit has to bring up to our remembrance.

I have personally experienced this flow many times while I am ministering. In fact, this flow usually sums up some of my favorite services. When I teach in Bible school or seminary settings, notes and

outlines are many times requested because the students need reference material, sometimes to prepare for exams. But even with that
setup, I intentionally make room for a flow of inspired utterances to
pop up! I have seen that these inspired, unplanned messages many
times are a demonstration of the mercy and foreknowledge of God in
ministering to the need represented in the room. I see these sudden
swerves in the services as a divine interruption of our plans for the
meeting, and we should all want the Spirit to interrupt our meetings!
My plan for the service aims to minister to everyone. But I love when
the Spirit zeros in on specific situations, persons, and emphases!

*The anointing teaches us by bringing up timely truths that we have known
or should know!*

Taught by Illumination

The second way that the anointing teaches us is by divine illumination. This is to say that God opens the eyes of our spirit so that we
see what was previously hidden or only seen partially. This might
include giving us thoughts, ideas, and understanding that we had not
previously had. While this many times manifests quietly, with the still
small voice of the Spirit teaching us, I have also seen when God has
randomly sent someone my way to say something that answers or
expounds a thought I'd been having. This has even happened when
I inadvertently overheard a conversation. The illumination from the
Spirit is really a spark of divine light shining on an area that He wants
to teach us about.

> **The illumination from the Spirit is really a spark of divine
> light shining on an area that He wants to teach us about.**

Years after Jesus had told the disciples that the Gospel was to be
proclaimed to all the world, the early Church still interpreted that

to only be all of the Jewish world. They were hearing the charge of the Great Commission through their limited social lenses. They were not preaching the Gospel to Gentiles and were unsure that they even needed to.

Through a series of unfolding trance visions, the Spirit began stirring the waters of Peter's very restrictive understanding of Jesus' command. The visions did not contain illumination of the Great Commission, but they did prep Peter's heart.

> *Now while Peter **wondered within himself what this vision which he had seen meant**, behold, the men who had been sent from Cornelius had made inquiry for Simon's house, and stood before the gate* (Acts 10:17).

> ***While Peter thought about the vision**, the Spirit said to him, "Behold, three men are seeking you"* (Acts 10:19).

The Holy Spirit is a gentle Teacher! He will prepare our hearts for the lessons He wants to teach us!

The vision captured Peter's attention and opened the way for Peter to see God's true intention for all mankind. While at Cornelius', a Gentile's, home, Peter's heart was illuminated and he understood: **"God has shown me** *that I should not call any man common or unclean"* (Acts 10:28).

The visions got Peter's attention and started him thinking, but in the end, "God has shown me." Peter said nothing of an external, audible, or observable occurrence that lead to his new understanding of Gentiles. Peter simply said, "God has shown me."

This key teaching that Peter had illuminated to him by the Spirit opened the way for Gentiles to be accepted in the Church, which means that many of us today are enjoying the benefits this illumination the Spirit taught Peter!

The anointing teaches us by showing us things we have been unable to see.

A similar stirring to know more about God happened with the Ethiopian eunuch. A man of some financial and political importance, this eunuch also had an interest for the things of God. On a trip *"to Jerusalem to worship"* (Acts 8:27), he was drawn to read a messianic passage in Isaiah 53:7-8. The Spirit arranged it:

> *Philip ran to him, and heard him reading the prophet Isaiah, and said, "Do you understand what you are reading?"*
>
> *And he said, "How can I, unless someone guides me?" And he asked Philip to come up and sit with him. ...Then Philip opened his mouth, and beginning at this Scripture, preached Jesus to him* (Acts 8:30-31,35).

In this instance, God arranged for the eunuch first to have a pondering hunger about a passage of scripture, then supernaturally arranged for Philip to catch up to his chariot so that his Spirit-inspired hunger could be satisfied with the true interpretation of scripture, pointing him to Jesus as Messiah. God does not just provide answers, but in wanting us to arrive at truth, the Spirit of God will many times inspire necessary questions so we can receive the necessary answers.

In Matthew 16:13-19, Jesus did this with the disciples when He asked them who they thought He was. The revelation Peter received of Jesus as the Christ was a result of the question Jesus led him into to begin with. God is so good; He feeds us the questions we didn't know to ask so He can give us the answers we didn't know we needed! God is the source of every good thing!

What happened with the Ethiopian eunuch is an example of how God can send people your way to answer a question that He inspired in you. The anointing that teaches you is also the same anointing that can guide you to places or people through whom you can receive answers and illuminations. Conversely, the anointing can guide you to places to bring an answer to others.

How will you know if what you hear and from whom you hear is right and from God?

Besides the obvious, that what is spoken has a scriptural basis, the anointing within you will witness to the validity of what you are hearing. The anointing guides, teaches, and protects!

The anointing guides, teaches, and protects!

I know that in my life, as a young kid growing up in Asia, God sent specific ministries across my path in the form of their ministry products like books, magazines, and recorded messages. This was before you could have access to a multitude of ministries on the internet, and being a kid in Asia, there were not many conferences or meetings I could get to. I had a hunger for God, and since I was the first one in my family to be born again and Spirit filled, there really wasn't anyone I could talk to.

Years later, when I started going over to America and would get in meetings and pray and fellowship with different ministers, on more than one occasion they'd comment that they could recognize the flow and the sounds of the Spirit through me. They would ask if I had got in on many meetings and were always surprised when I said that I had not. Teaching and impartations of the Spirit only fall on hungry hearts and can be transmitted through any means God sends!

Eyes Opened to Know

The opening and illumination of our spiritual eyes is only possible through an operation of the Spirit in our lives. Our natural minds and study methods can give us head knowledge, but it takes a touch of God to have our spiritual eyes enlightened, flooded with the light of the Spirit.

We cannot see the glories of heaven with the light of the world. Only the light of God can light the way to God!

> **We cannot see the glories of heaven with the light of the world. Only the light of God can light the way to God!**

This is why the Word of God alone cannot lead anyone to God. It takes the active involvement of the Spirit. This does not mean it has to be a dramatic demonstration of the Spirit's Presence, but it takes at least the silent, inner work of the Spirit for the Word to come alive and bring life to the reader. Both the Word and the Spirit together are required to bring us to the things of God.

If all it took was the Word alone, then anyone who has ever stayed in a hotel room with a Bible in the nightstand should have been born again! I am always heartened to see a Bible in my hotel room nightstand. In fact, I always check for it when I am in a hotel. On occasion, I've been led to lay hands on those Bibles and to pray for the Spirit to speak to the next hotel guest in that room through its pages.

Another way that we can say that the anointing teaches us is that *the anointing illuminates us to truly see what we may have been looking at for a while.*

This is exactly what happened to the two disciples on the road to Emmaus. The early disciples' dismay at Jesus' crucifixion was soon overshadowed by excitement as word spread that Jesus' body could not be found in His tomb. Some of the disciples were unsure what to make of all this. Several miles outside of Jerusalem, two such disciples, Cleopas and Simon, were engaged in a spirited conversation; *"they conversed and reasoned"* in excited tones about all these happenings

(Luke 24:15). Yet, tellingly, their intellectual pursuit of truth did not yield any revelatory results. Jesus approached them but their eyes were restrained from recognizing Him (Luke 24:16); both His physical form and true spiritual self stayed closed to them. Rebuking them for having closed minds and hearts, Jesus:

> Beginning at Moses and all the Prophets, He expounded to them in all the Scriptures the things concerning Himself. ... Then their eyes were opened and they knew Him; and He vanished from their sight (Luke 24:27,31).

Jesus vanished from their physical sight after they had gained spiritual sight of Him because their spiritual sight and recognition of Him was more important than their physical sight of Him. Physical sight of Jesus was no longer necessary when they had their spirits illuminated to have spiritual sight of Him. This is true of us modern-day believers as well. In John 20:29, Jesus told Thomas, "*Because you have seen Me, you have believed. Blessed are those who have not seen and yet have believed.*" Believing in Jesus, as Cleopas and Simon found out, was a result not just of having the scrolls of scripture opened, but their eyes opened as well. This evidently was an act of the Spirit because they later recounted to one another, "*Did not our heart burn within us while He talked with us on the road, and while He opened the Scriptures to us?*" (Luke 24:32). Their heart burning within them was a witness of the anointing within guiding them as they were taught the scriptures.

So far, we have seen that Paul had an *annoyance* with the girl with the python spirit of divination, then he *perceived* that there would be a shipwreck, and now Cleopas and Simon have their *heart burning within*. All these describe inner sensations of our spirit man that the anointing gives us in communication for our growth and guidance.

Taught by Teachers

Third, the anointing leads us to and teaches us through the ministry of those called to teach in the Body of Christ. We will look in a later chapter at the anointing on the office of a teacher.

In many ways, the teaching ministry was my first encounter with the Protestant world after I got born again. Of course, since I grew up Catholic, I did not know there were different branches within Protestantism. The anointing within guides us to such ministries that the Spirit knows we have need of because not only does the Spirit raise up anointed teachers but He also knows which ones we need in our lives.

Individually, no one believer does, but collectively, the Body of Christ has access to all of the anointing aspects of the ministry of Jesus. The Body of Christ together has the potential to represents the full ministry of Jesus on the earth. So while the anointing within us is able to teach us, the full measure of the anointing is found through the anointing that is already on the earth realm, on others.

By the design of God, the gifts and the accompanying anointings are spread out throughout the Body of Christ. This means we need each other for the full flow. Pointing back to the Day of Pentecost, in Acts 2, when the 120 disciples gathered in Upper Room, the blueprint for the flow of the Spirit was obedience and unity.

God set it up intentionally so that no one ministry, no one movement, no one organization will "have it all" and be able to function fully independently without need or regard for other parts of the Body of Christ. This is why there are seven gifts mentioned in Romans 12, nine in 1 Corinthians 12, and five in Ephesians 4. God intended for there to be diversity in the gifts and anointings. There is no one who can claim *full* maturity and *complete* proficiency in *all* these manifestations and anointings. Every ministry and believer will be more fluent in some of the gifts and anointings than they will be the others. Part of this is because of the calling of God on their life, but a lot of development in the anointing is also about yielding to that flow. The more we yield, the more skilled we get! We have some access to all the diversity of the anointing since we all have the same Spirit, but because of gifts, callings, and maturity, we will be more yielded and skilled in our particular function in the Body then in others.

As I remember it, in high school when we were in a math class, we did not study physics, and when we were in physics class, we didn't study history. But when the classes were all put together, we had enough of an education to graduate! This is how it is in the spirit as well. There will be different teachers, ministers, for different "classes," and one isn't better than the others. They all have their place and impartations to add to the Body!

I have used this same illustration when I occasionally hear people accuse other ministries of not being "balanced" or not "preaching the full counsel of God."

This is why the anointing teaches us through anointed teachers and ministers He sends our way. We're not designed to just study with our Bible in a coffee shop alone somewhere! Of course, God can and does speak to us when we study alone, but when we do, we only have access to the individual anointing; we cut ourselves off from the anointing on others and the corporate anointing! We need both the individual and corporate anointing!

We know which teachers we are supposed to study under in the same way we know which people to get involved with in life—by the go, stop, red light, green light, peace, no peace anointing guiding us! That same anointing will guide us on the truth of what we hear and direct us to the right teachers we need. In my life, I have also seen that God will send different teachers and ministers across my path depending on my seasons and needs as I grow in Him.

But He Also Teaches Us Directly

Last, even though we just got through talking about how we need others in the Body of Christ, it's also true that the Holy Spirit teaches us directly. There are two ways the Holy Spirit does this.

One way He does this is to speak to us directly and privately. This can be during our worship, prayer, and study time, or it can be just as we are going about our everyday life.

Then the other way the anointing teaches us directly is that as we are listening to someone teach, preach, or talk, the Holy Spirit can speak inwardly to us but above and beyond what they are saying, so that it's not just the voice of the person ministering to us that we hear, but we hear the voice of the Holy Spirit louder than and beyond them. You could say we hear the one ministering with our physical ears while simultaneously hearing the Holy Spirit with our spiritual ears. And the Holy Spirit could likely say something that isn't even related to what the minister is preaching about. Or the Holy Spirit could amplify what is being said, taking it to a level that is totally beyond what is taught. It is like seeing beyond the seeing and hearing beyond the hearing!

I have both experienced this type of communication from the Holy Spirit and have received multiple testimonies of others who have experienced this at meetings in which I have been ministering. You could say they walked away from the service with a whole different outline from what I preached!

The main difference between this personal way the anointing teaches us and the previous way we talked about, through the ministry of teachers, is that the former teaches by illumination from instruction and the latter teaches illumination by intimacy.

In a way, with this second method that we have looked at, the anointing teaches us when we set ourselves to get in His Word through study and in His Presence through prayer. That is communication through our yielding to the prompting of the Spirit, because we only want to study and pray in response to hearing Him call. This may not be a loud or direct call but, rather, many times an inner, gentle nudging.

However, there are also times when, without our initiation or our participation, the anointing jumps into the midst of our day and instructs us!

The difference between this fourth way the anointing teaches and the second way, when the anointing illuminates our study time, is intentionality. In the second way, we are intentionally studying to hear God and have Him teach us. In this fourth and last way, the Spirit speaks over what we are hearing and doing as we go about our life.

A big part of the anointing in teaching us directly is that it builds and trains us in communication with the Spirit. The Spirit seeks communication so that our lives can be guided and protected in the ways of God, but primarily it is so we can have ongoing communication. God's goal is that we have a personal relationship with Him! Communication and intimacy are important to the Spirit, and you cannot have one without the other.

So while guidance and direction are a big part of the Spirit's ministry toward us, His main ministry is to dwell in us and in doing so, restore our sonship (Romans 8:19). God seeks reclamation and dominion on the earth through His sons and daughters!

Communication from and to God, in and through our everyday life, is an ongoing reminder that God is with and in us.

We have a right to assume that if He is with us, God would be communicative. Conversely, it would be a shame to have God with us and then not allow Him a voice. So regardless of which way we look at this, it is within reason to say that God intends to speak! This is the basis of the anointing within—God wanting to speak.

The role of the Holy Spirit as Teacher and Guide is made available to our lives by His Presence. We recognize this Presence as the anointing.

When the anointing teaches us, it is because we have developed an intimacy with the Spirit, enough to allow and recognize His voice. The start of this is to be quick to obey the inner promptings, the green and red light sensations that arise as the anointing guides us. Having the anointing teach us is a stepping stone to the path of knowing the voice and Person of the Holy Spirit. It is a level of intimacy that can only be the result of gradual, regular interaction.

I believe that today, all over the world, the Holy Spirit, by the anointing, is walking with believers through their own roads to Emmaus so that they can know what who He is and what His role is in their lives. It takes the Spirit to show us the spirit realm. It is the anointing that is our "spirit realm garment." The anointing cloaks us spiritually and is both our covering and how we are identified.

The function of the anointing is not just the "sound in the spirit" but it is also what tunes us to that sound. So it is not just the equipment we need to function in the spirit realm but it is also what trains us to function in the spirit.

The anointing is vital in the life of a believer because the anointing is what God has bequeathed to the Church in the age we live in!

I still have many things to say to you, but you cannot bear them now (John 16:12).

CHAPTER 4

ANOINTED FOR LIFE

In these initial chapters of the book, we've looked at some basic ways that the Holy Spirit works in our life toward our growth. I consider this to be only a very introductory overview of how His Presence, manifested as the anointing, works in our life. Yet although this is not a comprehensive work, I consider this an important work, both to instruct and inspire a new generation that is hungry after God but also as a record of what I have learned of God so far. The Holy Spirit is God, and as God it will take us all of eternity to know Him fully. Yet He has ordained that it is now, in this earth realm, that our relationship with Him begins. This makes our time on earth precious because God has ordained for it to be the start of our relationship with Him—a relationship that will last for eternity. This is what significance in this life is—that we can step into eternity from it.

Our first visit to the spirit realm should *not* be after we shed this earthly body. As far as God is concerned, we are *already* seated in heavenly places in Christ (Ephesians 2:6). To be seated next to Christ is to be seated high up in the spirit! Since we are still on the earth realm, all that needs to happen is that our soul—which is comprised of our will, emotions, intellect, memories, and imaginations—and our body need to catch up with where we already are in the spirit.

To have a relationship with the Holy Spirit demands that we allow Him to lead us. It would be similar to saying "Jesus is Lord" but then we remain chiefly in control of our lives. He could *not* be Lord if we are the ones who determine everything without even a thought of inquiring of Him! *That is what separates the converts from the disciples. One believes in Jesus to gain eternal life; the other one follows after Him to begin eternal life now!*

That same understanding must roll over to our relationship with the Holy Spirit. He is God in us and on the earth and so must be given preference over all, including ourselves. *To say that Jesus is Lord is to also say that the Holy Spirit is Lord!*

If we want to know Jesus, we'll need to know the Holy Spirit. To know the Holy Spirit is to know His wants and His ways. To know His wants and His ways is to know and flow with the anointing.

The anointing, then, is very simply the vehicle by which the Spirit shows up in our life.

The anointing is not *just* for the emergencies of life any more than the Holy Spirit is!

Before the ascension, Jesus promised, "*Lo, I am with you always, even to the end of the age*" (Matthew 28:20). How is Jesus going to be with us always? Through the Holy Spirit. So the Spirit and His accompanying anointing are to be with us *always*. This was Jesus' promise and the Holy Spirit's mission.

For sure, the Spirit's anointing is available in times of need, but to *only* draw from the anointing during those times would be to choose to live a life without the power of God the rest of the time. That is actually part of the reason why believers falter when facing seemingly Goliath-sized challenges. Like David, we need to train in the anointing with the lion and the bear so that we're ready for Goliath. Had David not successfully overcome the lion, he would never have needed to be concerned about the bear because the lion would have eaten him!

An Anointing for Every Battle

No temptation has overtaken you except such as is common to man; but God is faithful, who will not allow you to be tempted beyond what you are able, but with the temptation will also make the way of escape, that you may be able to bear it (1 Corinthians 10:13).

God in His mercy only allows progressive giants! As He did with David, it is the plan of God that we train into facing the lion by looking after the sheep in our lives. Overcoming the lion qualified David to face and overcome the bear. Overcoming the bear trained David toward conquering Goliath. With each challenge, there was enough grace from God to conquer. All David needed to do was step up as each challenge presented itself to him.

God in His mercy only allows progressive giants!

This is why learning the flow of the anointing in our regular everyday life is important. Like David, we can learn to faithfully yield to the Holy Spirit daily as we tend to the "sheep" in our life. David never guessed that being faithful in the rather monotonous daily routine of shepherding was actually his God-ordained training for the lion, then the bear, and finally Goliath! When we are faithful in the "small," everyday tasks of our lives, God qualifies us for more. Cooperating with the flow today trains us for victory tomorrow!

There is a basic principle of seedtime and harvest that God employs in all that He does with us. If we will steward the seed that God puts in front of us, being faithful to plant and water it, then allow for time to develop that seed, God will bring us into a season of harvest. Our preparatory training for the loud demonstrations of the anointing is seeded in our private, quiet, hidden times when no one sees us.

The love of God seeks demonstrations through us, His Body, so that those around us might know and experience Him.

53

The wisdom of God teaches us first in private, away from the public eye, so that we will not just burn bright with the Spirit as His witnesses but we will finish our race well and burn all the way through the night!

The wisdom of God teaches us first in private, away from the public eye, so that we will not just burn bright with the Spirit as His witnesses but we will finish our race well and burn all the way through the night!

The Holy Spirit is also a gentle spirit. He teaches us both gently and gradually. He is gentle in that He does not ever force us and gradual because He teaches us upward from where we are in life and our spiritual walk.

Walk in the anointing every day and you will never meet a mountain too big for you!

To walk in the anointing every day is part of the process of renewing the mind that Paul teaches about in Romans 12:2. The renewed mind is in essence the mind of God, and the anointing is in essence the actions of God. One is the result of the other because actions follow thoughts.

The renewed mind is the mind that is trained to act and react the way God would, which is to act and react in the anointing.

Training our mind with the Word is freeing our spirit to the anointing!

Knowing what the Word of God says opens our mind up to what is possible in God. So the renewed mind is aware of and receptive to the anointing.

Flowing in the anointing without a renewed mind leads to self-destructive, kooky behavior and ultimately opens the door to the possibility for familiar spirits to operate. A renewed mind is what keeps a believer grounded in the fundamentals of discipleship. It is destructive when believers operate out their natural mind or wacky emotions but insist it's the anointing leading them.

It is only the renewed mind that is able to discern and *"prove what is that good and acceptable and perfect will of God"* (Romans 12:2).

This is why the previous aspects of the anointing that we have looked at are important—leading, teaching, and guiding. When believers try to skip forward to the demonstrations of power without allowing the anointing to grow them, it tilts them off-balance.

> *When believers try to skip forward to the demonstrations of power without allowing the anointing to grow them, it tilts them off balance.*

An unrenewed mind is not familiar with the genuine moving of the Spirit, nor can it flow with the anointing. I have seen unrenewed minds manifest in an untold variety of ways around the things of the Spirit. Believers whose minds are not renewed think being brash, rude, and offensive is an "authoritative prophetic anointing"! An unrenewed mind blames everything on demons so that they do not need to take responsibility for their lives. An unrenewed mind is more fascinated by the gifts of the Spirit than the fruit of the spirit. An unrenewed mind has a "magic unicorn" version of the Holy Spirit— they tag "the Spirit told me" to any sentence they imaginatively make up so they can impress those around them. The list could go on. An unrenewed mind lives a natural, painfully carnal life but is not concerned enough about that to allow a real encounter with both the Word and the Spirit of God.

The Anointing Is the Will of God!

> *And do not be conformed to this world, but be transformed by the renewing of your mind, that you may prove what is that good and acceptable and perfect will of God* (Romans 12:2).

The leading of the Spirit is continually seeking to guide us toward the will of God. And intrinsically, the will of God for us is always answered in the anointing! Since it is the anointing that destroys the yoke of bondage, since the anointing is the manifestation of the Spirit of God, there is no answer we need that is not found in the anointing!

The depth of the anointing we allow in our lives leads us to the "good, acceptable, and perfect will of God." The more we allow the leadership of the Spirit, the deeper into the anointing we will swim!

Learning to follow the leadership of the Spirit should really be the primary goal of every believer. *The alternative to being Spirit-led is to be self-led!*

How the Spirit Leads

Since the Spirit of God lives on the inside of us, that's the primary location from which He speaks to us. This is why understanding the anointing within us is such a vital part of our walk as believers. Hypothetically, it is possible to live a basic, normal, everyday Christian life without demonstrations of the Spirit and power. They wouldn't be fully effective, reach their full potential of being a witness, or be a force demons have to reckon with, but they could live a daily Christian life and make it into eternity. The same cannot be said of believers who crave for or have demonstrations of the Spirit and power but don't develop an awareness of the anointing within. That power of the Spirit without the balance of the anointing within a believer guiding, leading, and teaching them would soon lead to a short circuit and burn those around them. It would be irresponsible to talk about the power of the anointing without emphasizing a need for true intimacy with the Holy Spirit, a walk of holiness, a working knowledge of the Word of God, and to allow for the fruit of the Spirit to develop in us.

I have met 19-year-olds who told me that they were going to write a book about the Holy Spirit. I told them they needed to *read* a book about the Holy Spirit, not write one! I spend time on a regular basis with young people to mentor and teach them about the Holy Spirit. I have witnessed firsthand the things God can and does do through young people. I am a firm believer in investing in the next generation of believers. Of course, God can and does speak to 19-year-olds. And of course, they have a testimony to tell their peers and the world. But a relationship with the Holy Spirit, like any other relationship, takes time to develop and deepen.

The same can be said for a relationship with the Word of God. It takes time for fruit to mature! We give the enemy unnecessary access when we prematurely push younger believers to positions that their inner life with God cannot sustain. Obviously, the same can be said of people who have been in church longer but still haven't matured. We should not assign anyone a position in church just because they've been members for a long time! Spiritual growth and a walk with God are important to Him!

Occasionally, I'll come across believers who are fascinated with giving personal words of prophecy to others. It's true, we are told to *"desire earnestly to prophesy"* (1 Corinthians 14:39), but Paul also told us that we *"prophesy in proportion to our faith"* (Romans 12:6). We know that faith comes by hearing the Word of God (Romans 10:17). So this means faith grows, which means that our propensity to prophesy grows. Anything that grows moves from immaturity to maturity. I would rather have a "mature prophecy" than an immature one! I have counseled such believers many times, and besides the basics we've already discussed, I told them to get with someone who is more mature in moving prophetically so that they can be mentored and discipled in that flow of the Spirit.

Strangely, a while ago I came across a lady who claimed that she wouldn't have a quick lunch with friends when invited after church unless the Holy Spirit wanted her to go. Her perplexed friends never knew if she wouldn't eat with them because she was busy or if God did not want her to hang out with them! Equally disturbing, I got to know of another lady who seemed to have a propensity for God telling her who her single friends' future spouses were going to be! She never told them who specifically but always gave them a mysteriously knowing look, saying, "The Spirit showed me who, but I can't tell you."

All of this adds up to nothing but a puffed-up mystical air of spirituality that is neither necessary or fruitful. The Spirit might caution you against going to lunch with someone on a rare occasion that calls for it, but generally God does not need or want to micromanage and dictate who you have lunch with! You are free to choose! The Spirit is also not tale bearer. He is not a gossip. Why would the Holy Spirit reveal to someone else, who was neither a spiritual elder nor a more mature believer, who you are to marry? Wouldn't God at least draw your attention and attraction to the spouse He has planned for you before He tells someone else who you are going to marry without you even knowing? And even after God does draw your attention to someone and a potential relationship starts to bud, why would God tell the end result of that courtship to someone else? There is no anointing to be a busybody!

We need to realize that because the Holy Spirit is God, He is also a Spirit of order because God is not the author of confusion (1 Corinthians 14:33).

Having a move of the Spirit with demonstrations of power may look chaotic to the natural eye as it did on the day of Pentecost, but the divine order of referring to the Word of God first was still immediately implemented by the Holy Spirit who inspired Peter to reference Joel to explain what had happened. There is a system of divine checks and balances that God has put in place to safeguard the manifestations of the anointing.

Led to Sonship

> *For as many as are led by the Spirit of God, these are sons of God. For you did not receive the spirit of bondage again to fear, but you received the Spirit of adoption by whom we cry out, "Abba, Father." The Spirit Himself bears witness with our spirit that we are children of God, and if children, then heirs—heirs of God and joint heirs with Christ, if indeed we suffer with Him, that we may also be glorified together* (Romans 8:14-17).

So when we see that the anointing is not just demonstrations of power but the divine ability to live a strong, long, godly life, we move from just believing and expecting for divine demonstrations of power to standing for divine representation of the God-kind of life.

This is what the Spirit is always leading us toward. The Holy Spirit is always leading us upward, back toward the Father. The Holy Spirit always leads us home as sons and daughters.

In John 10:10, Jesus made a statement that has rightly been often quoted in an evangelistic setting, presenting a salvation message: "*I have come that they may have life, and that they may have it more abundantly.*" Some have left this to mean Jesus came to give us eternal life—and that is true. But the word for *life* that Jesus used here is the Greek word *zoe*, which *Vine's Complete Dictionary* tells us is used in the New Testament of life as a principle, life in the absolute sense, *life as God has it, that which the Father has in Himself, and which He gave to the incarnate Son to have in Himself!*

So the abundant life that Jesus intends for us is not just eternal life or length of life but a certain type, a particular quality of life. That quality of life is as God Himself has it! The intention of God in sending Jesus was that we literally have the God-kind of life! This was only possible by a divine Blood transfusion made available on the Cross of Calvary!

The sons of God are the *only* ones in whom the Spirit of God their Father can dwell. Thus, the sons of God are the only ones through whom the indwelling Spirit can manifest! This is the Spirit's main goal in His ministry of teaching, leading, and guiding us—to bring us toward Christlike sonship.

Christ Formed in Us

My little children, for whom I labor in birth again until Christ is formed in you (Galatians 4:19).

You may have noticed that, for the most part, among those who are not believers, there is reasonable acceptance of "Jesus" in the world. You often hear all kinds of politicians, athletes, or entertainment personalities—who otherwise show no real interest in having Jesus as Lord of their lives, or even in trying to live by scriptural principles—talking about "Jesus" or thanking Him when they receive an award or win something. They'll talk about how Jesus loved and accepted everyone. I am not talking about new or growing believers. I am talking about individuals who express no immediate intention to be a disciple of the Lord in any way.

The name *Jesus* is rightly sacred and certainly all-powerful to us as believers because we know the Man whom the name represents. We know historically that there were others also named Jesus. In New Testament times this name was common among Greek-speaking Jews. In fact, when offered by Pilate, the crowd chose to have Jesus Barabbas (Matthew 27:16), a condemned criminal, released instead of Jesus Christ.

We also know that *Christ* was not Jesus' last name. It was not as if there was Joseph Christ, his wife Mary Christ, and then their son,

Jesus Christ! *Christ*, from the Greek *Christos*, was a prophetically bestowed title meaning "anointed, Messiah."

I certainly am not attempting to separate "Jesus" from "Christ," since we know Jesus *is* the Christ. But for the sake of clarity in this teaching, it is worth pointing out that while many in the world who don't personally know Him, may tolerate "Jesus," it is the "Christ," the anointed Messiah side of Jesus, that they have no tolerance for. It is the "Christ-side" of Jesus that was anointed to do all the miraculous plundering of the enemy's kingdom in setting the captives free. It is the "Christ-side" of Jesus that is an affront to everything that the forces of darkness stand for! It is the "Christ-side" of Jesus that sets us free from the bondage of sin and death! Christ, literally, is the *anointed* Messiah!

It is therefore no coincidence that Paul labored in prayer and ministry that "*Christ* be formed in you"! Paul's ministry was pointedly toward Christ, the *anointing,* being formed in us! The anointing formed in us is what constitutes maturity in our sonship. This is why it is not enough to just have an experience with or even be around the anointing. If we are to grow in our sonship, into Christ-likeness, we must grow in our awareness, sensitivity, and yield-ability to the anointing!

The early disciples were first called *Christians* in Antioch (Acts 11:26). Tellingly, this was not what they called themselves, but was coined by non-Christian Gentiles. Although *Christ* is Greek, -*ian* is a Latin addition. This suffix means "of the party of." So the early disciples, as followers of Jesus, were identified by the surrounding community as Christ-the-anointed-One followers. There was something about the early disciples that caused those who were not believers to see Christ the anointed One in them! They demonstrated Christ the anointed One by living an anointed lifestyle. Through their lifestyle in the anointing, Christ in turn lived through them.

The anointing is the manifest demonstration of God's will and ways through His sons and daughters on the earth realm.

The anointing is what enables us, on earth, to reflect and represent our Father in heaven.

The anointing is a cloak of divinity on our body of mortality.

The anointing is a cloak of divinity on our body of mortality.

Illustratively, I have said it this way: our spiritual birth certificate is signed in the Blood of Jesus and our spiritual driver's license is signed in the anointing of the Spirit!

I received this saying from the Spirit, through tongues and interpretation: the anointing requires recognition because the anointing requires cooperation, and you cannot corporate with what you do not recognize!

Obedience Is Better

The next time you get a prompting to give—yield!

The next time you get a prompting to reach out to someone—yield!

The next time you get a prompting to spend more time in the Word—yield!

The next time you get a prompting to pray—yield!

The power of God, the anointing, is released only as we yield! Yielding to the promptings may seem like a sacrifice at that moment, but that is only because the natural mind does not see what the Spirit has planned for us in reciprocity to our yielding to the anointing.

I remember once, years ago, as my day began, I headed out to run some errands. As I was heading into my first appointment, I sensed the anointing within bubbling up in an unction to pray. I was so focused on my meeting that I chose to ignore it and instead whispered to

God, "God, I will gladly give You three hours of uninterrupted attention in prayer later tonight when I am back home!" Later that day, when I was done with my errands and back home, I tried "giving" God my three hours of uninterrupted prayer, and it was the deadest, longest three hours of praying I had ever experienced! The "prayer time" dragged on like a burdensome dead weight tied to my back! Near the end of that unction-less prayer time, I heard the Spirit quote 1 Samuel 15:22:

> *So Samuel said: "Has the Lord as great delight in burnt offerings and sacrifices, as in obeying the voice of the Lord? Behold, to obey is better than sacrifice."*

I had tried sacrificing three hours to God in place of a moment of yielding to the anointing within in prayer! I tried forcing God to accept my three hours of my flesh-effort, sweat-soaked praying offered entirely in my own strength, in place of my rejection of the Spirit's offer to corporate with the anointing within and yield. Obedience in better than sacrifice because there is always a grace and an anointing that flows on and though us as we yield to the Spirit. The next day, reflecting back to that experience, I went before the Lord about it and repented. He spoke to me and said, "Obedience is better than sacrifice because if you will obey, you do not need to sacrifice!"

In obedience, there is actually not a sacrifice because we always end up with more than we started with. That is not a sacrifice, that is a gain! What is truly a sacrifice is when we lose out on God's best through obedience and then have to settle for the fruit of our own disobedience! Partnering with the anointing and receiving God's best is never a loss or a sacrifice! The anointing never leads us to loss!

Initiated by the Spirit

When I look back to some of the richest times of my spiritual growth as a believer, I realized it was actually always a result of my accepting an invitation of the Spirit. It was never something that I initiated but rather always by the initiation of the Spirit. Sometimes in my immaturity, I had thought I initiated something that led to my growth, like studying the Bible or prayer. But even in those basics, they were really silent promptings by the Spirit in my spirit that I responded to. In my own self, I had no ability to want God. He drew me. Even in our receiving of Jesus as Lord and Savior, it is the Spirit who convicts us of the truth of the Gospel (John 16:8).

I have found that maturity in the things of God involves recognizing that God is first and rightly the source of all good. The work of the Spirit, through the functioning of the anointing, affects us in more ways than we have ever known.

The more we lean in on the functioning of the anointing in our lives, the closer we get to the life God intended us to have.

SECTION 2

THE ANOINTING TO GO

CHAPTER 5

SALT AND LIGHT

You are the salt of the earth. ...You are the light of the world. A city that is set on a hill cannot be hidden. ...Let your light so shine before men, that they may see your good works and glorify your Father in heaven

(Matthew 5:13-14,16).

God's purpose in teaching, guiding, and developing us personally into mature sons and daughters is that God through us will have representation of Himself in this earth realm.

As we have already seen, the anointing goes deeper beyond demonstrations of power, but that is not to say that the anointing should not also go wider so that it affects those around us.

As it is with anything that has to do with God, the anointing is strategically purposeful. It is not just so we can get warm, fuzzy feelings. No doubt, the anointing touches and heals our emotions, but the anointing is not just so we can have an emotional experience. *The essence of the anointing is that we, the children of God, can be employed and empowered to express the life of God on earth.* As with everything else that God does, the anointing starts working inside us before it manifests outside us.

When the world rejects—and, in my opinion, rightly so—what they see as antiquated, obsolete Christianity, it is really their rejection of powerless, theorized Christianity. In other words, Christianity that is "all talk and no action." Clearly, the Church should be involved in "good works"—humanitarian outreaches that better society and communities. I believe that the Church should lead the field, but the Church is not the only organization that can offer humanitarian help. Many other organizations, secular and religious, do as well. What sets the Church apart from any other organization is that the Church has the ability to set the captives free (Luke 4:18)—and that takes the anointing!

The Church moving outside of the anointing of the Spirit simply downgrades itself to the status of mere humanistic men.

Sent Like Jesus

So Jesus said to them again, "Peace to you! As the Father has sent Me, I also send you" (John 20:21).

The power of the anointing accompanies us as we are sent. *To be sent implies we are directed to go and not just that we decided on our own to go.* The power of God is resident in the commands of God. This means that as we obey His commands, the anointing, which is the power to cause that command to come to pass, goes with us. I remember hearing this old saying when I was a kid in church: "Some were called and some were sent. Others just bought a microphone and went!" The supply of the Spirit is only available on the paths of the Spirit! It is important to understand that although we are sons and daughters of God with access to the fullness of the Spirit, the Presence of the Spirit cannot be dragged along in our life at our whim and fancy. He has to lead and guide. The Holy Spirit invites and guides us into our destination. He will not be strung along into our fantasies!

I have met successful businessmen who assumed that their success in business meant they could also pastor a church, and I have met effective pastors who decided that success in ministry was a clear sign they should start a business. I have seldom seen it not end up a mess when they decided to leave their realm of calling and authority and branch out by their own desires into another vocation. Now, I have met and know personally some who are equally successful in both ministry and secular endeavors, but that was always by the specific leading of the Lord and not just by the convenience of opportunity. He supplies His grace when we stay in our place! This is why what we have previously looked at—the Spirit leading, guiding, and teaching us—is vital as the initial and ongoing development into our walk in the anointing. *There is no anointing outside of His leading!*

To be sent clearly implies that a communication is initiated, received, and responded to. It is crucial we understand that it is only with the commands of the Spirit that the anointing of the Spirit is available. In many ways you could say that learning how to hear the voice of God and having a relationship with the Holy Spirit is senior to learning about the anointing itself. As we have said, the anointing comes with His Presence, so we are to be pursuers of God and not just pursuers of the anointing.

I first had the Spirit teach me from this verse many years ago. I remember that the first time I ever preached it was in a small ministry school in the Philippines that had about 12 pastors in attendance. It was so fresh to me because I had just had the Lord show me the week before that Jesus Himself did not come into ministry on earth by His own will but by that of the Father. And because Jesus was responding in obedience (Hebrews 5:8-10), the Presence and the accompanying anointing rested on Jesus.

How Jesus Was Sent

When He was teaching me about this, the Spirit lead me back to study how Jesus was sent, commissioned out to public ministry.

Now, we know that Jesus was the Lamb slain from the foundation of the earth (Revelation 13:8), but when He finally incarnated onto the earth, Jesus then had to walk out that plan. In this, as with all else, Jesus remains our example on how to walk out the plan of God. So how was Jesus sent?

Initiating the beginning of His public ministry, all four Gospels record the baptism of Jesus by John.

> *Then Jesus came from Galilee to John at the Jordan to be baptized by him. And John tried to prevent Him, saying, "I need to be baptized by You, and are You coming to me?"*
>
> *But Jesus answered and said to him, "Permit it to be so now, for thus it is fitting for us to fulfill all righteousness." Then he allowed Him.*
>
> *When He had been baptized, Jesus came up immediately from the water; and behold, the heavens were opened to Him, and He saw the Spirit of God descending like a dove and alighting upon Him. And suddenly a voice came from heaven, saying, "This is My beloved Son, in whom I am well pleased"* (Matthew 3:13–17).

Before Jesus publicly announced His ministry, He submitted Himself to the baptism of John. Just like He left the glories of heaven to be on this paltry earth, this act of baptism was the Greater submitting to the lesser. Jesus did it over John's protest. John knew by the Spirit who Jesus was and so knew that he had need to be baptized by Jesus instead of it being the other way around. Yet Jesus insisted. This was obedience to the Spirit and humility before mankind displayed! Just as Jesus would later submit to Calvary despite having no sin, Jesus now submitted to John's baptism despite having nothing to repent of.

From this position of obedience, Luke's Gospel records that Jesus prayed (Luke 3:21). So we see that prayer came after obedience, which came after following the prompting of the Spirit. Luke goes on to say that while Jesus prayed the heaven was opened. To have heaven open up as Jesus prayed would point to it being closed before He prayed. Prayer opens heaven! More specifically, prayer from a position of obedience opens heaven to us! We cannot pray away disobedience nor can we pray from disobedience. The only remedy to disobedience is to submit and obey.

Once the heaven opened, the Spirit descended symbolically as a dove upon Jesus. So again we see what obedience, or yielding, makes available to us. The Spirit only lands on yielded vessels! With the Spirit upon Him, Jesus heard a Voice from Heaven with a sure but reassuring tone, "*You are My beloved Son; in You I am well pleased*" (Luke 3:22). This precious portion of scripture showcases all three members of the Trinity.

With this announcement from Heaven, Jesus was declared God's beloved Son, in whom God was well pleased. Yet this was before Jesus had done any mighty works. Jesus had not yet raised anyone from the dead, cleansed any leper, or miraculously multiplied food. *God's pleasure with us starts at the point of our obedience, submission, and yielding to the Spirit.* It is not *just* what we accomplish with the anointing that causes God to be pleased with us, but it is that as sons and daughters we position ourselves to hear and follow after Him submissively. The anointing, what it enables us to do, and what we do with the anointing is not what grants us acceptance before the Father. *It is our heart posture that opens heaven to us!* This is primary in our study of the anointing; God does not supply us with the anointing so we can *perform for* Him. God supplies us the anointing so we can *be like* Him! God's heart is to have sons and daughters—not just servants!

Luke 4:1 goes on to record, *"Then Jesus, being filled with the Holy Spirit, returned from the Jordan and was led by the Spirit into the wilderness."* The faithfulness of God saw to it that Jesus was filled with the Spirit *before* the wilderness. Jesus did not go into the wilderness with an empty tank! If we will keep our hearts tuned to seek the Lord, God never allows a wilderness challenge in our lives that He does not first fill and empower us for! It is never God's intention that we be blindsided by the enemy. God has a filling and an anointing to see us through every wilderness experience! *The anointing doesn't just empower us but it can also preserve and sustain us.*

The Spirit only led Jesus into the wilderness for the confrontation with the devil to demonstrate to us how a Spirit-filled, Spirit-led, anointed child of God could encounter and be victorious over any circumstance. Jesus led the way to show us how to face the enemy head-on and come out victorious. Jesus met and silenced the devil in each of the three wilderness encounters with the Word of God! We see how the filling of the Spirit and the accompanying anointing manifested through Jesus in the wilderness—Jesus had immediate recall of an appropriate Word for each challenge as it came His way! Jesus was anointed to speak the Word! Often we think of the anointing in demonstration as a dramatic healing or deliverance, but we should not forget that the anointing can also manifest by bringing us a word to speak!

This wilderness confrontation was a direct demonic attempt to prevent Jesus from walking into His earthly ministry. The anointing does not just wait to meet us at the place God has called us to but the anointing can protect, guide, and bring us to that place! We can trust the Spirit every step of the way!

After this victorious encounter, *"Jesus returned in the power of the Spirit to Galilee, and news of Him went out through all the surrounding region"* (Luke 4:14). So there was a *filling and leading* of the Spirit before Jesus entered the wilderness, *manifestations* of the Spirit while Jesus was in the wilderness, and demonstrations of the *power* of the Spirit when Jesus return to Galilee. Jesus was never alone through this entire ordeal. The anointing is not just for refreshing times when believers have corporate gatherings but is also available in the wilderness when we are alone!

Jesus dramatically described His call of being sent from God in the synagogue with a quotation from Isaiah 61.

> *The Spirit of the Lord is upon Me, because He has anointed Me to preach the gospel to the poor; He has sent Me to heal the brokenhearted, to proclaim liberty to the captives and recovery of sight to the blind, to set at liberty those who are oppressed; to proclaim the acceptable year of the Lord* (Luke 4:18-19).

Again, we see that the Spirit of the Lord being on Jesus resulted in Jesus being anointed. The Presence and activity of the Spirit is not separate from the functioning of the anointing in a person's life. The Holy Spirit is manifested as the anointing, and the anointing is evidence of the Spirit's Presence!

Before this announcement, we have no record of Jesus doing any miraculous works publicly. If Jesus needed the anointing to walk into His call, how much more do we? We see that the subsequent works Jesus did were not done just because He was divine but rather as a Man anointed by the Spirit. Yet again, this was in demonstration and an example for us. If Jesus only operated in the miraculous because He was a member of the Godhead, that would leave all of us out since we are not divine. But because Jesus, while on the earth realm, operated as a Man anointed by the Spirit, He showed us all the way we too could operate! This is why Jesus was able to send and commission us in the *same* way He was sent! *We are sent to go forth in the anointing, and in that anointing is the divine ability to function as Jesus would in any situation!*

Isaiah prophetically summed up how Jesus was sent. Jesus, in turn, said He was sending us that same way! It would be accurate, as one sent in the same way Jesus was sent, to claim and speak this prophecy over ourselves.

In Luke, Jesus outlined the functions of the anointing that rested on Him—and now rest on us!

Isaiah's Catalog of the Anointing

First, Jesus was anointed "to preach the gospel to the poor." *Gospel* means good news. What could be good news to the poor except that they need not be poor anymore? The anointing has the ability to break the stifling grip of insufficiency and lack over a person's life. The entrance of the Gospel in any region, historically and internationally, is the precursor to advancement and betterment of that society. There is something about the Gospel that brings light and freedom to people, not just spiritually but materially. This does not mean that the Gospel makes everyone who is a follower of Jesus a multimillionaire. But it does mean that children of God have a right to expect God to supply *all* their needs according to His riches in glory by Christ Jesus (Philippians 4:19). To be fully supplied means that I have enough to take care of my needs, the needs of my family and loved ones, and have enough to give into and support the work of God. The anointing can destroy the yoke of lack!

This anointing is not limited to geographic locations. I have seen this in operation in many third-world villages that I have preached and pioneered in. It would never be long, once there were believers in that region who got a hold of the message that the anointing could deliver them from lack, before we would start to see material increase come to them. Like we all do, they had to operate in the principles of giving in order to enter into a cycle of receiving, but once they knew that destroying lack was a function of the anointing, they could add faith to their giving.

Healing the brokenhearted is the next function of the anointing that Isaiah listed. This speaks of healing for our emotions and memories. It is a very limited understanding of God's healing anointing to think that God only heals physical bodies. If God were to *only* have healing available for our physical bodies that would mean that God only intends to have one-third of our being healed and whole since Paul teaches us in 1 Thessalonians 5:21 that we are a tripartite, three part, being, comprised of spirit, soul, and body. Our soul is our will, emotions, intellect, memories, and emotions.

For some, the healing touch of the anointing on their emotions is all that is required to have healing in their bodies. I have also seen people who were crippled as adults, mentally and emotionally, because they were brutally traumatized and abused as children, be set free as the anointing healed their inner brokenness. Of course, choosing forgiveness and renewing their mind were involved in their deliverance. But as in the case of understanding that the anointing can destroy the yoke of lack, they first had the anointing touch their broken heart, then they were set free enough to begin the process of restoration. Today, in a culture that is broken and confused about so many things, we need this aspect of the anointing more than ever!

The Anointing Proclaims

Third, the anointing is available to "proclaim liberty to the captives." This speaks of an anointing to declare the good news of freedom to those bound. *Proclaim* is from the Greek *kerusso* (Strong's G2784). *Vine's Expository Dictionary* says this "signifies to be a herald; to publish; to preach." This means there is an anointing to preach! Primarily this means to preach the good news of salvation, but this preaching anointing does not just stop at salvation. Since this anointing to preach is identified by the proclamation of liberty, we can deduce that the anointing to preach and proclaim can bring us to liberty in all areas of life!

The fruit of this aspect of the anointing is that people get set free. *It is really easy to gauge if preaching is Spirit-led and anointed—the hearers get set free from the bondage of old mindsets, old habits, old fears, and enter into a new level of intimacy with the Spirit of God.* Preaching that produces fear, confusion, and an unhealthy dependence on the minister is bondage, not liberty. That is *not* a function of the anointing.

Just as the healing anointing is not limited to just heal bodies, the anointing to proclaim is not limited to pulpit preaching. The function of the anointing is not just to raise preachers but to raise up those who will proclaim the Gospel—and the Gospel should be proclaimed not just from the pulpits but from the boardrooms to the classrooms!

As with all aspects of the anointing, there is more than one shade to this function. So the healing anointing is not just for healing evangelists, and the preaching and proclaiming anointing is not just for preachers on a Sunday morning! You see this wide spectrum of variables with all manifestations of God. In the spiritual gift of prophecy (1 Corinthians 12:10), for example, that prophetic utterance could come to the believer by them hearing a word from the Spirit, seeing an inner image, having a vision, a dream, or even having a word bubbling up from within them. There is no end of ways that one particular operation can manifest! This is simply because each manifestation of the anointing is an actual entry of God Himself into the physical realm and there is no way to contain God to a predetermined, fixed form!

An anointing to proclaim liberty to the captives—that is, anyone who has not yet received Jesus as Lord and Savior—is available to any believer who will take to heart Jesus' command to go into all the world and preach the Gospel. So if a businessman, housewife, or student will accept that as a believer they have a responsibility to be a proclaimer of the Gospel, then in their everyday interactions this anointing will flow and make room for them to proclaim Jesus.

As we obey the command to go into all the world and proclaim the good news, we can fully expect this anointing to be in manifestation (Mark 16:15). *The Gospel is a supernatural message to produce a supernatural result and can only be delivered and received by supernatural means!*

Next, the anointing, as outlined by Isaiah, brings "recovery of sight to the blind." Beyond seeing the opening of blind eyes in the ministry of Jesus, I believe this speaks to a deeper operation of the anointing in the opening of spiritual eyes closed to the things of God. As Elisha prayed for his servant's spiritual eyes to be opened (2 Kings 6:17), Paul would later pray for a similar result in the Ephesians that *"the eyes of your understanding being enlightened"* (Ephesians 1:18). It takes the anointing to open the eyes of unbelieving mankind because it is the god of this world, satan himself, who has blinded them (2 Corinthians 4:4). Spiritual blindness affects all who reject or oppose God's offer of salvation through Jesus' sacrifice. There is an aspect of this anointing that speaks to the plundering of the enemy's kingdom in giving sight to the spiritually blind so that they no longer stay confined through lack of sight. I believe this is a summarily vital operation of the anointing because having a person's spiritual eyes open and accepting the Gospel is what births them into the Kingdom.

We see an example of this anointing in manifestation at Jesus' baptism when John, seeing Jesus approaching, declared, *"Behold! The Lamb of God who takes away the sin of the world!"* (John 1:29). We know this was not just a mental or emotional conclusion on John's part but a spiritual awakening because later, outside of this anointing in operation when John was in prison, his natural mind started wondering and he sent his disciples to ask of Jesus, "*Are You the Coming One, or do we look for another?*" (Matthew 11:3).

The same happened to Peter, who had a revelation of Jesus as the Christ and made the confession, not of flesh and blood, but by revelation of the Father (Matthew 16:13-19). Then later, at the arrest of Jesus, in moments of desperate fear and confusion, Peter would go on to deny even knowing Jesus personally, much less by revelation in the spirit (Luke 22:54-62)! It takes having spiritual eyes open to see Jesus for who He is, because evidently, like with John the Baptist and Peter, the natural mind rejects the revelation of Jesus as Christ.

But again, this function of the anointing giving sight to the blind can be broadened. To be sure, Jesus Christ is Lord and Savior, but He is not just Lord and Savior to get us to heaven. He is also potentially Lord and Savior of our finances, our physical ailments, the Baptizer in the Holy Spirit, our Deliverer, and so much more. I say "potentially" because I know from experience that everyone who receives Jesus as Lord is not always immediately open to receiving Him as Healer, as Provider, or as Deliverer. Jesus will only be to us what we allow Him to be, and that takes our spiritual eyes opening to see Him in His majestic fullness, not just one aspect of His ministry toward us. This is where anointed teaching and preaching are vital to bring illumination of the Word by the Spirit. The delivery of the Word in an environment of the Spirit's anointing opens blind, religious eyes to the fullness of the Gospel!

Paul reinforces this idea in Romans 10:14-15:

> *How then shall they call on Him in whom they have not believed? And how shall they believe in Him of whom they have not heard? And how shall they hear without a preacher? And how shall they preach unless they are sent? As it is written: "How beautiful are the feet of those who preach the gospel of peace, Who bring glad tidings of good things!"*

A Confrontational Anointing

Equally confrontational to the kingdom of darkness is the next function of the anointing in Isaiah's catalog: *to set at liberty those who are oppressed.* Since we also know from Isaiah that the anointing destroys the yoke, the yoke, then, must have been placed by the enemy to enslave. Or, if the enemy did not fasten it on directly, then the enemy at least makes the yoke temptingly available so that mankind enslaves himself.

While we should rightly see and approach the anointing from the perspective of God's manifest Presence, we should not forget that the anointing also equips us to dissipate darkness by being the light of God. This means that the anointing in manifestation is in direct conflict with the devil's devices of enslavement. We are equipped in the anointing, not just to replicate God's works on the earth but to disarm the enemy as well. This means we are armed for war! In spiritual warfare, we are not fighting *for* victory but we are fighting *from* victory because Jesus has already defeated the enemy for us! We are simply enforcing the enemy's defeat with the authority that God has bestowed us.

On one side of the spiritual warfare ditch is the idea that *everything* is a demon. If you were late to an appointment, it was a demon. If you misplaced your keys, it was a demon. If you overate, it was a demon. The other ditch is where, because we are now in modern times, demons no longer exist or are active, so everything can and should only be analyzed and resolved from an intellectual, humanistic perspective.

Neither of those two ditches are scriptural. The middle ground, the scripturally balanced approach, is that we do need to take personal responsibility for our life, build ourselves up in the things of God, keep our body under control, and strive toward a lifestyle of excellence. On the other hand, we need to recognize that there is a spiritual realm and there are both forces of good and evil that seek to have influence over us. You cannot cast out the flesh, and you cannot discipline a demon! But the anointing can enable you to discipline the flesh and cast out demons!

Now to be clear, God and the devil are *not* in some sort of eternal wrestling match. God is God, creator of heaven and earth, high above anything that the devil could ever be. God is the creator and lucifer was but a creation. God is the Almighty and satan is but a rebel. God did not create satan, but lucifer became satan after he fell. There is nothing of the devil that even compares to God for there to be a cosmic contest of any kind. What the enemy cannot do to God, he tries to do to the children of God. *The anointing is our stamp of heavenly authority by which we can arrest and expel the enemy!*

To *set* is the Greek word *apostello* (Strong's G649); setting at liberty those who are oppressed carries the idea of setting apart, to put in, to go to an appointed place, even to order one to depart. So the anointing can very purposely set a captive into liberty.

This is a function of the anointing that I have seen in operation many times in my ministry. The results have always been glorious! One example that comes to mind was when I was wrapping up a series of revival meeting that had produced much fruit for the Kingdom. On the last night, as the congregation was down at the altar and rejoicing over all that God had done, I noticed that at the back of the hall, the crowed seemed to be clearing a small circle around a man. I saw that this man had picked up a chair and was swinging it about wildly. At that moment, he looked up and we locked eyes. He started spitting and screaming at me. I couldn't hear him nor he me, because the hall we were in was a big hall and the people down front were singing and praising God loudly. I sensed the anointing come on me and I said above a whisper, "Peace! Be still!"

Many times I sense the anointing as a wave, and this time I sensed a wave of that anointing hit the man in the back of the hall. He suddenly froze and fell over backward, stiff as a board. I finished the meeting and about two hours later, as we were leaving, I noticed that he was still lying on the floor where he had fallen over when the anointing had hit him. On the way to the airport the next afternoon, I asked the pastors who came to get me about him. They told me that he worked for one of the local elders at church and didn't remember much of what had happened the night before. They excitedly told me that when he finally was released from the anointing and got up near midnight, his left foot, which had been turned inward since his childhood, had been straightened out! As a young child, his parents had brought him to a temple and dedicated him to the local deity. A week after, his foot turned inward and he had been crippled ever since. He left church delivered and healed! He was a captive whom the anointing set at liberty!

Last, Isaiah, declares that the anointing is available, "*To proclaim the acceptable year of the Lord.*" Tellingly, Jesus stopped short of quoting the verse in full. If Jesus did, it would have ended with "*and the day of vengeance of our God*" (Isaiah 61:2). But instead Jesus declared that the anointing would declare the "acceptable year of the Lord." The anointing enables us to invite mankind to respond to God's offer of partaking in the acceptable year of the Lord. What is the acceptable year? Every year since the death, burial, resurrection, and ascension of Jesus has been an acceptable year of God to receive His offer of salvation!

Even if Jesus had quoted the full verse, it was a *day* of vengeance as opposed to an entire *year* of acceptance! The psalmist said it this way, "*For His anger is but for a moment, His favor is for life*" (Psalm 30:5). We do not have an angry God! He is merciful and kind! The anointing will *always* speak of receiving God's favor because it is the goodness of God that leads us to repentance (Romans 2:4). The anointing will always point to our good God because there is no mean, vengeful God!

I Also Send You!

These five general aspects of the messianic anointing were announced by Jesus as a public declaration of His mission and function. It formed a skeletal blueprint for what He was to do. None of these functions were possible without the anointing. It took a supernatural empowerment to accomplish the mission of Jesus—and it still does. When Jesus commissioned us to go as He went, it was with the full understanding that it took the power of God for us to do so. The anointing on the Person of Jesus is now still on the Body of Christ!

CHAPTER 6

BAPTIZED IN FIRE

The anticipation of the Messiah was a topic that captured all of Jewish culture. For as long as they had existed, the Messiah had been promised to them and was all they looked for. Now that the early disciples had seen and experienced Jesus, they were raring to present Him as the Promised One. It must have surprised them a little when instead of sending them forth to herald His coming, Jesus instead told them that they needed to wait, that their time with Him was not enough for them to enter the world as witnesses.

In our previous chapter, we saw how Jesus began the process of announcing His public ministry with submitting to John's baptism.

Historically and scripturally, baptism always implied an immersion. Matthew records that "*When He had been baptized, Jesus came up immediately from the water*" (Matthew 3:16). That Jesus *came up* from the water means He was first *down in* the water. You could not ever get up from a baptism dry, like you did going in. You would have physical evidence for all to see of what you had been submerged in.

There are always three components to a baptism. First there is the baptizer, then the baptizee (the one being baptized), and finally the substance in which the baptizer immerses the one getting baptized. A baptism demonstrated a person was being completely submerged, drenched, and engulfed in the substance used. No part of the person being baptized was left untouched. A true baptism always resulted in a complete saturation.

There also has to be a certain level of trust between the baptizee and the baptizer because the baptizee has to believe that the baptizer will immerse him in the necessary substance, not leave him in there, but then take him out at the appropriate time.

In Matthew 3:11, John the Baptist made an unusual prophecy about Jesus: *"I indeed baptize you with water unto repentance, but He who is coming after me is mightier than I, whose sandals I am not worthy to carry. He will baptize you with the Holy Spirit and fire."*

This was an aspect of the Messiah that had not been articulated by any of the previous prophets till now! The people understood being immersed in water, but to be immersed in the Holy Spirit and fire? There was relatively little revelation knowledge of the Holy Spirit under the Old Covenant since almost no one qualified to have access to the Spirit outside of the prophets, kings, and priests.

Jesus picked up on what John said about the Holy Spirit and provided the disciples with clear directives.

> *Behold, I send the Promise of My Father upon you; but tarry in the city of Jerusalem until you are endued with power from on high* (Luke 24:49).

> *But you shall receive power when the Holy Spirit has come upon you; and you shall be witnesses to Me in Jerusalem, and in all Judea and Samaria, and to the end of the earth* (Acts 1:8).

Just as John made it known that he would be baptizing with water so people could respond, Jesus was now making known to His disciples that He would send the Promise of the Spirit. In essence, Jesus was announcing when and where He would be fulfilling John's prophecy of baptizing the disciples in the Holy Spirit!

A Little Bit About Baptisms

Because we want to grow and mature in the things of God and flow with proficiency in the Spirit, scriptural clarity on terms and ideas we have is important. Without clarity, confusion and uncertainty abound. This has certainly been the case with the things of the Spirit. I believe there are many people who are hungry for or at least curious about spiritual things but haven't taken the time or had the opportunity to study it scripturally.

If you have been around Spirit-filled church circles at all, you would have undoubtedly heard the phrases *being baptized with the Spirit, receiving the gift of the Spirit,* and *filled with the Spirit.*

Typically, these terms are all used to describe the same event of the Day of Pentecost in Acts 2:4. Actually, while the scriptural references are correct, the reason there are three terms to describe the same event is because there are three separate individuals involved in this one occurrence.

First, Jesus is the One baptizing us with the Spirit.

Second, we are the ones receiving the Holy Spirit.

And last, the Holy Spirit infills us.

Looking at the topic of baptism, it would serve us to know that the Word actually speaks of more than one baptism. Hebrews 6:2, speaking of foundational, elementary doctrines, mentions "*of the doctrine of baptisms*" in the plural.

There are actually three main baptisms that are described in the Word.

Baptized into the Body

Although they are actually different, we also commonly use the terms *baptism **of** the Holy Spirit* and *the baptism **with** the Holy Spirit* interchangeably.

85

For by one Spirit we were all baptized into one body—whether Jews or Greeks, whether slaves or free—and have all been made to drink into one Spirit (1 Corinthians 12:13).

The purpose of baptism was obviously not that the baptizee would be drenched with water but really it was for identification. In a way, even with water baptism, it was similar to an anointing because the baptized person was publicly set apart, consecrated to a specific way of life and purpose.

This is the first and the most important of the baptisms—the baptism *of* the Holy Spirit—because this baptism results in our eternal salvation. This is the one baptism Paul was referring to in Ephesians 4:1-6:

I, therefore, the prisoner of the Lord, beseech you to walk worthy of the calling with which you were called, with all lowliness and gentleness, with longsuffering, bearing with one another in love, endeavoring to keep the unity of the Spirit in the bond of peace. There is one body and one Spirit, just as you were called in one hope of your calling; one Lord, one faith, one baptism; one God and Father of all, who is above all, and through all, and in you all.

Paul here was talking about salvation. And there is only one baptism that saves us because this is what actually happens when we accept the sacrifice of Calvary.

At our new birth, when we receive Jesus as Lord and Savior, the Holy Spirit as the Baptizer takes us, the baptizee, and baptizes us into the Body of Christ (Romans 6:2-4).

Through this baptism, we are immersed into the Body of Christ. We then arise, alive in Him, as a new creation!

After this initial, all-important baptism, then either the second or third baptism can happen in no particular order.

One of these other baptisms is water baptism. Water baptism can take place any time after a person believes on Jesus.

Baptism with the Spirit

The other is the baptism *with* the Holy Spirit. This baptism can take place before or after water baptism. We see this with the new Gentile believers in Acts 10 who received the Holy Spirit and started speaking in tongues but had not yet been water baptized.

As we saw, in the first baptism, a believer is submerged in the Body of Christ by the Holy Spirit. This is spiritually significant and is a witness to the spiritual realm, God, and the angels and demons that a person is now consecrated and set aside to God. Potentially, he is then baptized in water by the physical, local church. Water baptism is a witness to the local, physical Body of Christ, friends, and family that a person has officially, publicly made a confession of faith in Jesus.

In the third baptism, fulfilling John's prophecy, Jesus, the Baptizer, takes us, the baptizee, and immerses us in the Holy Spirit. Thus, we are baptized *with* the Holy Spirit.

This is what Jesus wanted His disciples to wait for in Jerusalem before they headed out to be witnesses for Him. John said that Jesus would baptize with the Holy Spirit and fire (Matthew 3:11). Jesus added to that and said that they would be *"endued with power from on high"* (Luke 24:49) and *"receive power"* (Acts 1:8). Piecing this together, the fire and the power of the Spirit to be witnesses are synonymous! Jesus did not plan for any witnesses to be without Holy Spirit fire! And of course, *since fire equals the power of the Spirit and the power of the Spirit equals the anointing, we can then conclude that the fire also equals the anointing!* So in essence, Jesus did not want the disciples attempting to obey His command to go into all the world without the fire, the anointing of the Spirit! The anointing is necessary for us to go to our world!

This is exactly what happened in the Upper Room on the Day of Pentecost—the Holy Spirit filled the whole room that the disciples were in, so in essence they were submerged in the Spirit, and there appeared the fire John had prophesied, as divided tongues on each of them!

The Witnesses Start Witnessing

Of course, one of the main talking point of the Pentecost Upper Room account is that the disciples, as they were filled with the Holy Spirit, all started speaking in tongues. This is crucial to our understanding of the anointing of fire because it was only after this that any kind of witnessing was accomplished by the early Church. With the baptism of fire, the early Church started displaying the miraculous signs of the Spirit that accompanied the ministry of Jesus. With this baptism in the anointing, they now started walking in the supernatural abilities that Jesus had in His earthly ministry. They were empowered with heavenly abilities and could now respond to situations like God would!

I once asked the Spirit why it was that at such a crucial juncture of the Church, the physical body part that He affected was their tongue and not their hands or feet. He immediately reminded me of the third chapter of James:

> For we all stumble in many things. If anyone does not stumble in word, he is a perfect man, able also to bridle the whole body. Indeed, we put bits in horses' mouths that they may obey us, and we turn their whole body. Look also at ships: although they are so large and are driven by fierce winds, they are turned by a very small rudder wherever the pilot desires. Even so the tongue is a little member and boasts great things.

See how great a forest a little fire kindles! And the tongue is a fire, a world of iniquity. The tongue is so set among our members that it defiles the whole body, and sets on fire the course of nature; and it is set on fire by hell. For every kind of beast and bird, of reptile and creature of the sea, is tamed and has been tamed by mankind. But no man can tame the tongue. It is an unruly evil, full of deadly poison (James 3:2-8).

Our tongue is the rudder of our life. It sets the direction of our life. *The words we speak determine the ceiling of what we have faith for. We cannot be in faith if we are speaking doubt!* We cannot believe for life when we are speaking death! Our tongue affects us in a circular manner—the words we speak are not only an indication of what our heart is overflowing with, but the words of our mouth will also fill our hearts (Romans 10:8-10). So we speak what we believe and we'll end up believing what we speak.

Life and death are released by the words we speak, and yet no man has ever been able to tame the tongue. So in enabling the disciples' natural tongues with a heavenly language, the Holy Spirit was rerouting the direction of their lives toward their heavenly calls. *The Holy Spirit gave them supernatural tongues to steer them toward a supernatural life!* The Holy Spirit Himself did not speak in tongues but they spoke *"as the Spirit gave them utterance"* (Acts 2:4). So they cooperated with and yielded to the Holy Spirit to release a heavenly manifestation on the earth. This is exactly how the anointing works. The anointing will always require our yielding to produce. Speaking in tongues, yielding our human tongue to a heavenly utterance as the Spirit provides, is an immediate, daily way we can practice yielding to the Spirit.

Undoubtedly, part of what the 120 disciples prayed and declared as they spoke in tongues was that they would walk into their call to be a witness as Jesus had commanded. And as the rudder of their tongue directed, just as James said, their lives followed! *When the Holy Spirit set their tongues on fire, He set their lives on fire!*

Just like at Jesus' baptism, it was a personal, supernatural encounter that set the stage for a public ministry. Three thousand men were born again on the day of Pentecost. The flow of the Spirit in the Upper Room overflowed onto the streets and the disciples became witnesses!

Tongues of Revelation

Actually, in Acts 1:8, Jesus had said the disciples would receive power when the Holy Spirit came on them, yet when this was actually fulfilled, what the disciples immediately received was the ability to speak in heavenly tongues. So we can say that the heavenly tongues was a demonstration of the Holy Spirit fire and power that Jesus spoke about! Why? Because the heavenly tongues changed the trajectory of their lives—and that is what the anointing does!

Speaking in tongues is not just for special occasions. Tongues are for our everyday lives. It is no coincidence that Paul, who was not part of the original twelve disciples, ended up writing nearly three quarters of the New Testament because he revealed, "*I thank my God I speak with tongues more than you all*" (1 Corinthians 14:18). So Paul evidently lived in a continual flow of heavenly communication and, in doing that, was well trained to yield to the anointing. What Paul finally wrote down, which we have as the New Testament, was really just the result of his spirit man being yielded and trained to the anointing. *When our tongue is trained in the flow of the Spirit, our lives will follow!*

Much of what Paul recorded in the epistles he wrote was such deep revelation that even Peter, who was one of the original twelve disciples, said his writings were "*hard to understand*" (2 Peter 3:16). This means that Paul, who never sat under the earthly ministry of Jesus, knew more by revelation of the Spirit then those who had been in close physical proximity to Jesus' ministry! There is a flow of revelation available in the anointing that we can tap into!

Regarding this outpouring, Peter, quoting Joel, said, *"And it shall come to pass in the last days, says God, that I will pour out of My Spirit on all flesh; your sons and your daughters shall prophesy"* (Acts 2:17). As with the 120 disciples, the first sign that Joel and Peter, by the Spirit, identified as evidence of the outpouring of the Spirit was a verbal function—in this case, prophesying.

The anointing is a divine action on the earth realm.

The anointing is a divine action on the earth realm. All divine manifestations only occur after a divine utterance is made on earth. So God says what He will do before He does it. Always. This was the function of the prophets all through the Old Testament. They primarily had a recurring theme: the Messiah was coming. Why did God require so many prophets and so much time before Jesus incarnated? Because each utterance, once spoken by the anointing, works its way in the material, physical realm, moving toward manifestation and fulfillment. So because of the divine timing of God and the preparation of the people's hearts, it was necessary that a certain number of anointed utterances be declared on the earth so that the Anointed One could then step into the fulfillment of those declarations. Jesus came as fulfillment of prophecy, but those prophecies had to be uttered by and under the anointing first.

The anointing is the substance by which the manifestations of heaven are conceived, carried, and birthed on the earth realm!

The anointing is the substance by which the manifestations of heaven are conceived, carried, and birthed on the earth realm!

In giving the disciples a heavenly tongue, God was enabling sons and daughters who would prophesy—that is, be anointed to speak forth the plans of God on the earth—so that the plans of God could be conceived, carried, and birthed on the earth! This was a marked difference from the Old Testament in which only a select few could prophesy. Now, all believers can prophesy! Which means that now, all believers can be a start point or an add-on point to the unfolding plans of God on the earth.

In our learning about the anointing and the manifestations of the Spirit, it is *vital* to understand the place of learning to yield our tongues to God, simply because words are the beginning of any and all manifestations. It has been that way since Genesis: "And God said" proceeded any act of creation.

The realm of tongues is the realm of the supernatural flow that we can enter into, at will, any time. Learning to unhook from our head and operate out of our spirit is our master class to flowing in the anointing. And that is exactly what we are learning as we pray and speak in tongues. In entering into prayer and speaking in tongues, we are in effect choosing to yield to the prompting of the Holy Spirit in our spirit and speak from that location of the anointing.

> *The realm of tongues is the realm of the supernatural flow that we can enter into, at will, any time.*

The anointing on the Church to go into all the world is activated, not just by the Word of God that He has already spoken, but by our agreement with that Word. The only portion of God's Word that will work for you is the part you actively agree with. This is why God saw fit to have our tongues anointed. How else could we utter God's desires on the earth with just our natural speech birthed from our natural minds?

The anointing to go to our world in the power of God starts burning by the fire of God touching our lips! In our "going," we are actually being sent forth as prophesying ones. This is not to say we are all prophets but rather that we are going forth with a message from God.

Prophecy is not just foretelling but also forth telling! Both take the anointing of God. Both require a yielded heart and tongue.

Speaking in tongues is part of how we present our bodies as an acceptable offering to God (Romans 12:1). It is part of our consecration and separation from the world and unto God.

Pray Like Paul

After I got born again as a young teenager in Asia, the next major spiritual encounter I had was speaking in tongues. It was foreign to me because I did not grow up in a Spirit-filled church environment. But there was something about speaking in tongues that caused my heart to leap! As soon as I was filled with the Spirit, I spoke in tongues a lot. I would be about my regular day and be speaking in tongues. Many nights, I would pray though the early hours of the night speaking to myself in tongues in my little bedroom. I did not have the understanding of what speaking in tongues is or does. I simply did it because there was always such a sense of intimacy with God as I prayed. The Lord spoke to me once and told me that much of what I do today in ministry was first prayed and prophesied out in those times of prayer. Paul said that we speak forth mysteries when we speak in tongues (1 Corinthians 14:2). *The mysteries of God are kept for us, not from us!*

Anointed preaching and prophecy teaches and declares the mysteries of God to us. But the mysteries of God cannot be accessed by our natural mind or study alone. Those are good and necessary but are from a different realm. Our intellect, research, and study are from the realm of human reasoning, and these are based on data we feed it. Revelation from God, however, is from the spirit realm and comes to us not through our heads but through our spirits. It takes revelation for us to see the things of God! And it takes an anointing for us to receive revelation because it takes the Presence of God in manifestation speaking for us to hear Him!

In praying in tongues, we are really "prayer-prophesying." On one hand, we are praying and worshiping, speaking to God, and on the other hand we are declaring into our future. Basically, this is the essence of tongues. This is why praying in tongues opens the floodgates of the anointing. Not only is tongues a one-to-one conversation with God, but in that conversation we get to converse about things of the Spirit by the language of the Spirit.

Another benefit I have found with praying in tongues is that it continually keeps me aware of the Spirit's Presence in and with me, which in turn reminds me of the anointing! One way that Jesus fulfills His promise to be "*with you always, even to the end of the age*" (Matthew 28:20) is by the indwelling Presence of the Spirit.

An awareness of the Spirit cannot be separated from an awareness of the anointing. Knowing that we have access to the anointing should really be the beginning of our "going" into ventures of life and for God. Our "going" should really always be after our "sending"! The power is in obeying the sending! I have learned that in developing an awareness of the anointing, I have also learned to note when the anointing is not present!

A Gathering Before a Going!

Behold, how good and how pleasant it is for brethren to dwell together in unity! It is like the precious oil upon the head, running down on the beard, the beard of Aaron, running down on the edge of his garments (Psalm 133:1-2).

The anointing favors an environment of togetherness and unity. We saw this in the Upper Room on the day of Pentecost, "*they were all with one accord in one place*" (Acts 2:1). When we gather in one accord, we are acknowledging the other parts of the Body and so acknowledging the other portions and manifestations of the anointing.

Unity does not mean we put aside or compromise what we know to be true of God through His Word and His Spirit. Unity does not mean we all agree on all the same things in the same way. Outside of the necessary agreements on the very basic fundamentals of Christianity, like the virgin birth, the sinless life, crucifixion, resurrection, ascension, and deity of Jesus, we have room to come together lovingly, humbly, and respectfully as the family of God to research, study, and explore. Such a heart posture toward others in the Body of Christ honors God and opens our heart to receive from the anointings and deposits of the Spirit in other segments of the Body of Christ.

I have had the privilege of ministering quite widely across denominational and theological lines. Traveling internationally, I have noticed that even with those who hold to the same theological understandings, many times, because of culture and social surroundings, they express themselves very differently. When I first started accepting such ministry assignments from the Lord years ago, one of the things the Spirit helped me with was, "You are not there to bring the fire, you are there to add to the fire that is already there!" This helped shaped my understanding of cross-cultural ministry. I remember hearing how in the late nineteenth century, missionaries went to a remote region in Asia and preached the Gospel. They had some success, but they also carried their traditions with them. They instructed all the women to wear white after they converted to Christianity. This would not be an issue except that in that particular culture only the widows wore white. So for the women to be Christians, they had to walk away from much of the society that they knew and in effect walk around identifying as widows. The husbands were not thrilled, to say the least!

Our purpose in any of our "going" is to be vessels for the Spirit to minister life to people. That will ultimately bring change in society and culture, but that change cannot be enforced by our plans alone. That must be birthed and nurtured by the Spirit as the Word is proclaimed and established in that region. To be the salt and light that God intends us to be demands that we be agents of change, but that change must be birthed in prayer and the Spirit.

A proper understanding of unity will aid in the flow of the anointing as we go.

In our answering a call to go, part of what the anointing of God will give us is wisdom for where we are going to!

I have said the same thing to people who feel called to the business world. The anointing to start or be in a business will flow best if we allow for that anointing to also manifest as wisdom!

The anointing is tangible, practical spirituality! It is not all just goosebumps and tingly feelings!

Strife and discord in any matter, especially ministry related, are the devil's playground. It requires no faith if people are backbiting and politicking! And it takes faith to have the flow of the anointing! We would put aside anything that leads to disunity if we treasured and honored the anointing! When we see how costly the anointing is, we would not trade it for a petty argument!

> *For where envy and self-seeking exist, confusion and every evil thing are there* (James 3:16).

But strife does not just hinder the anointing; it opens the door to "every evil thing"! So strife is an usher—it ushers the anointing out and evil in!

When we honor the Body of Christ, we honor the anointing!

CHAPTER 7

OUR PROGRESSION IN THE ANOINTING

Jesus was a sent one. He was sent from the Father with a specific ministry for a specific people.

Jesus in turn sent the Holy Spirit. The Holy Spirit is sent with a specific ministry to specific people. To the world, the Holy Spirit's witness is that of salvation through Jesus Christ. To the Church, the Holy Spirit's ministry is that of guidance and empowerment.

There is divine order to the flow of the anointing.

Behold, how good and how pleasant it is for brethren to dwell together in unity! It is like the precious oil upon the head, running down on the beard, the beard of Aaron, running down on the edge of his garments (Psalm 133:1-2).

We looked a little at Psalm 133 in the last chapter. Although it is commonly referenced as a chapter on unity, we should also note that the anointing oil flowed first down the head, then the beard, and finally to the edge of Aaron's garments. This means that the anointing oil was not applied to Aaron's garment first; it was applied to his head first and flowed downward. There is order to how the anointing is applied and flows. Like with everything in the universe and in creation, God does not do anything without order.

Many times believers act as if the Holy Spirit is unknowable and erratic in all He does. They have an "anything goes so everything's right" attitude with the things of the Spirit. While it is true that our natural selves will not *fully* comprehend all the ways of the Spirit and that many times a demonstration of the anointing can cause unusual manifestations, it is not true that there is no order to the move of the Spirit. We may never have a full grasp of *all* the ways of the Spirit or how He will do something, but we can know enough of Him to be sensitive to Him. And if we are sensitive and tuned to Him, we will see that the Spirit moves progressively, for our sake, and He builds systematically. Besides the understood principles of never contradicting the Word and always pointing to and uplifting Jesus, how the Spirit moves, in part, is based on how much we have let Him teach us in previous encounters.

If there were no order, we could never learn the ways of the Spirit.

We know that Jesus Himself *"increased in wisdom and stature, and in favor with God and men"* (Luke 2:52). Jesus' 30 years before His public ministry were not just spent in idle obscurity but were times of development and growth. As we saw with Jesus' wilderness encounter, what Jesus did, He did as an example for us. As the Son of God, Jesus was already divine; as the Son of Man, He came to show us the way men could move in the things of God.

We see a definite pattern of progression in the miracles of Jesus' ministry.

Jesus' first miracle was that of changing water to wine (John 2:1-11). This was a miraculous working with the basic elements of the earth. It was not, in that sense, a "life or death" miracle. It was only after that, with Jesus' second recorded miracle, when Jesus started operating in ministering physical healing, involving the healing of the noble man's son (John 4:46-54). In this miracle, Jesus spoke and the child was healed *"at the same hour"* by His word (John 4:53).

We first see Jesus casting out demons when He was in the synagogue. One man with an unclean spirit was delivered (Mark 1:23-28; Luke 3:33-37). We don't see Jesus healing and delivering masses until later in Luke 4 (repeated in Matthew 8:16-17; Mark 1:32-34):

> *When the sun was setting, all those who had any that were sick with various diseases brought them to Him; and He laid His hands on every one of them and healed them. And demons also came out of many, crying out and saying, "You are the Christ, the Son of God!" (Luke 4:40-41)*

So we see Jesus moving from healing and delivering one to healing and delivering many.

The anointing through Jesus in raising the dead also manifested progressively. The first and second people raised from the dead under Jesus' ministry were the widow of Nain's son (Luke 7:11-15) and then Jairus' daughter (Matthew 9:18,23-25; Mark 5:22-23,35-43; Luke 8:40-41,49-56). In both of these instances, the ones raised had only been dead a short amount of time, likely a few hours. The next person raised from the dead was Lazarus, and he was dead four days before he was raised (John 11:1-44)!

We can grow in our skill and keenness by working with the anointing! Where we are now in relation to the anointing is not where we need to stay and is not all there is!

Signs Following Us

The anointing to go is an exclusive call to the Church. As with any divine call, there are divine signs that will follow if that call is answered.

> *And He said to them, "Go into all the world and preach the gospel to every creature. ...And these signs will follow those who believe:*

In My name they will cast out demons; they will speak with new tongues; they will take up serpents; and if they drink anything deadly, it will by no means hurt them; they will lay hands on the sick, and they will recover" (Mark 16:15, 17–18).

We see here five specific signs that follow us as we follow His sending:

1. Casting demons out. This is part of how we set captives free. Demons that had previously inhibited and controlled people can be cast out by the anointing as was demonstrated in the ministry of Jesus. Physical healing often accompanies the casting out of demons. The Lord showed me once that deliverance is a variant of the healing anointing.

2. Speaking in new tongues. This manifests in one of two ways. The first and the most widespread is when believers speak, pray, and worship in heavenly tongues. This is direct communication to God Himself, enabled by the Spirit. The other is when believers speak in a language that they have never learned and don't otherwise speak. The alternate manifestation of this is the interpretation of tongues in which the hearer recognizes or hears a language they understand even though a believer is speaking in a heavenly language. I have seen all these different manifestations in operation!

3. Authority over serpents when preaching. Serpents in this context could be one of two possibilities—actual snakes as Paul shook off in Malta (Acts 28:5), or it could demonic serpents/spirits. Paul also had an encounter with this when he cast the python spirit of divination out of the slave girl (Acts 16:16).

4. Immunity to poison. Supernatural protection is available to believers as they obey the plans of God. The protection of God is available when there are intentional efforts to harm us as well as when there are unintentional mistakes in consumption of harmful

substances. Elisha encountered poisoned stew and purified it (2 Kings 4:38-41).

5. Recovery of the sick through the laying on of hands. Healing has always been a hallmark of our Father! So it's a given that in sending forth the disciples, Jesus would specify that they had the authority to lay hands on the sick. Untold millions have encountered the love of Jesus through a healing touch administered through crusade evangelists and everyday believers as they obey this command!

Five Signs Through Nine Manifestations

The five signs that Jesus said would accompany believers are really the result of any one of the nine manifestations of the Spirit listed in 1 Corinthians 12:8-11. These nine all-encompassing manifestations of the Spirit are easily studied in three main categories.

The revelation gifts:

a. The word of wisdom: a revelation of the future to guide believers in a wise course of action. Agabus had a word of wisdom regarding a coming famine (Acts 11:28).
b. The word of knowledge: a revelation of facts present and past. Peter had a word of knowledge regarding Ananias (Acts 5:3-4).
c. Discerning of spirits: a revelation or discerning of the spirit world. Paul saw an angel of God with him (Acts 27:23-24).

The power gifts:

a. The gift of faith: a supernatural infusion of God's faith to receive a miracle. Daniel was protected from lions by a gift of faith (Daniel 6:10-24; Hebrews 11:33).
b. The working of miracles: a supernatural infusion of God's power to work a miracle. Samson, through the working of miracles, tore the lion apart (Judges 14:6).

c. The gifts of healings: a supernatural infusion of God's power to bring about healing and wholeness.

The vocal gifts:

a. The gift of prophecy: a message given by God to people in a known language through human vessels (Acts 15:32; 21:9).
b. Different kinds of tongues: a message given by God to people in an unknown language through human vessels (1 Corinthians 14:27).
c. Interpretation of tongues: an interpretation of the message given in tongues (1 Corinthians 14:27).

What we see very quickly as we study the anointing and the moving of the Spirit is that all His demonstrations are intricately connected and they lead us from one to another. There is a *system of the Spirit* in the flow of the anointing. The more we are intentional to let the Spirit teach us, the more we will see that there is an interlacing of His manifestations. Regardless of whether the outcome is healing, prophecy, or preaching, there are actually not many anointings but simply different operations and manifestations of the anointing, because there is but one Spirit from whom all manifestations flow! We often say a particular minister has a healing anointing or another believer has an anointing for business, but it really is obedience toward their call and boldness, together with consistency and intentionally toward the anointing that was necessary for them.

A Divine Knitting Together

From whom the whole body, joined and knit together by what every joint supplies, according to the effective working by which every part does its share, causes growth of the body for the edifying of itself in love (Ephesians 4:16).

We can be schooled in the anointing because the Spirit has specific roles for each of us in the Body. *The knitting must be by the Spirit so that the effective working can be by the anointing.* For growth in the Body, we require the flow of the anointing. I learned a while ago that individually I will not reach the whole world, but collectively the Body of Christ can. Every joint in the Body supplies, but every joint doesn't have the same function. It is important to have God lead and settle us in our function in the Body. We do not get to choose!

After I got born again, the church I was a part of had a great missions and soul-winning emphasis. I am always thankful for that because when I look back I see that even then, God was giving me an intentional vision. One of the things they did every weekend was to bus as many people from church as would show up down to the malls and shopping areas so they could talk to people about Jesus and invite them to church on Sunday. Because soul winning was such a big emphasis in the church, I got talked into going along one weekend.

Now, people who know me will know that I am very much an introvert. In fact, I always tell people that I am an introvert pretending to be an extrovert! If I were in a roomful of people and did not know anyone, I'd likely just try and find a seat at the back and stay there quietly, away from everyone else. All of this suddenly became real to me when I got off the bus and they handed me a stack of Gospels of John to go hand out and invite people to church! My palms got sweaty, I stammered, and I didn't make any eye contact with anyone. I went back on the bus to wait for everyone else as soon as I'd handed out my stack of Gospel booklets. I did this for a few weeks and was miserable every time!

I finally stopped going but felt guilty. The next year, I was on a missions trip to a neighboring country. Totally unexpectedly and through a long series of events, I ended up being asked to speak in a small church of about twelve people in the middle of a little village. Surprisingly, even though it my very first time speaking publicly, I did it without any strain and with much ease! I actually thoroughly enjoyed myself so much that I couldn't wait to do more trips! Some of the people on the missions trip were also on the witnessing bus and they were surprised at me! Then I found out that those who had great success witnessing one on one on the streets did not seem to have that same ease when they had to speak publicly. I was starting to find my place!

Whenever I share this testimony, I am quick to reiterate that while I am not at my strongest sharing the Gospel one on one, I still seek to obey God on the few occasions that I have felt the Spirit prompt me to do so. Finding your place in the things of God doesn't exclude you from other basic duties as a believer, but it does mean that you will be more inclined in certain giftings than in others. In what the Lord has had me to do around the world, many have been saved and healed not just in a corporate setting where I am ministering, but many have been witnessed to one on one from the different outreaches and ministries that have been started from our ministry efforts. We are the most fruitful in our *going* when we go where and how God sends us. The strongest measure of our anointing awaits us as we mature into the rooms and functions God has planned for us. God in His specificity and wisdom does not send us anywhere without already having first planned a definite role for us. This is why the anointing to go and do must be coupled with the anointing to hear and guide. Our doing is only effective in His guiding!

Man's attempt at self-placement and organization in the Church always results in dead religion because no anointing can accompany what God has not set apart! Administration and governance in any organization is necessary but only after the will of God has been sought and committed to as first priority. *It is the anointing that calls and accompanies a person for a position in the Body, but it is faithfulness and obedience that qualifies them!* The Spirit of God is seeking and raising up people who are not just full of faith but also faith-full!

Growing in the Anointing

Everything that God does in and for us, He does using the principle of the seed. This allows for us to grow anything that God gives us as much as we desire. The principle of the seed is simply that what is given by God is only and always in seed form and so must be planted and watered to grow. In the seed is everything needed for a harvest, which ultimately means more seed.

This principle of the seed also applies with the anointing. Our anointing can grow if we are diligent to tend to it.

We all receive the measure of faith when we are born again (Romans 12:3), but we also know that faith comes, meaning can increase in measure, by hearing (Romans 10:17). So if we turn our hearts and ears toward the written and spoken Word of God, we will increase in faith. Our faith can even grow exceedingly (2 Thessalonians 1:3)!

Since we prophesy in proportion to our faith (Romans 12:6), this would mean that as our faith grows, our propensity and ability to prophesy also grows. This could not just refer to prophecy but it must be a principle that applies to all the manifestations of the anointing. Jesus had even referenced the disciples' lack of faith as the reason why they were unable to function in the anointing as He had commanded them to cast out a demon (Matthew 10:1; 17:20).

We know that Stephen was full of faith and the Holy Spirit (Acts 6:5), and that was restated in verse 8 as Stephen being full of faith and power. If you can be full of anything, you can also be half full or empty! So as "full" of the Spirit as Stephen got was how full of power he was!

The anointing operates by faith. Since our faith can grow, it only makes scriptural sense that our anointing level can grow as well! *Grow your faith and your anointing will grow with it!*

Also, we see in Romans 12:6 that grace has been given to us in relation to operating in the manifestations of the anointing. Paul said that he *"became a minister according to the gift of the grace of God given to me by the effective working of His power"* (Ephesians 3:7). So there is a grace for each of us to function in the ministry God has for us. The grace of God on Paul to minister was deep and tangible enough to be perceived by James, Cephas, and John (Galatians 2:8-9).

Peter taught that grace could be multiplied and increased through our knowledge of Jesus (2 Peter 1:2). He also told us we can grow in grace (2 Peter 3:18). So like our faith can grow, grace can be increased in our life as well. And just like we operate in the anointing by faith, we receive the anointing by grace. Our operating in the anointing grows by faith and our receiving of the anointing grows by grace!

Because we can grow from grace to grace (John 1:16), for the sake of this study, we can also say that we grow from anointing to anointing!

This is why the life of a believer, involved in the things of God, is never one of stagnant dullness. Neither does being involved in the things of God drive one to "burn out."

God has ordained steps of growth for us, balanced growth, not just in doing supernatural works in the strength of the anointing but progressively as we grow in our faith and grace.

Like with faith and grace, the glory of God and the anointing of God are directly and proportionally related. When the anointing of God fills a place, the glory of God as a cloud is sometimes visibly manifested (Exodus 40:34; 2 Chronicles 5:14). In fact, it is the glory of God that causes people to fall under the power of the Holy Spirit. An increase in glory in our lives would definitely produce an increase in the anointing. Now if we are exhorted to grow from glory to glory, and since growing in glory produces growth in the anointing, then we should realize that we can grow in the anointing (2 Corinthians 3:18).

> *That He would grant you, according to the riches of His glory, to be strengthened with might through His Spirit in the inner man, that Christ may dwell in your hearts through faith; that you may be rooted and grounded in love. …Now to Him who is able to do exceedingly abundantly above all that we ask or think, according to the power that works in us* (Ephesians 3:16-17,20).

Paul prayed for the Ephesians who were already born again and baptized in the Holy Spirit to be strengthened with might, *dunamis* (Strong's G1411), which means "power" and is related to the anointing in their spirits according to the riches of His glory (Acts 1:8). Paul was actually praying for an increase in the anointing within, which is the believer's anointing, which in turn enables believers to go into the sendings of God!

We have therefore come to see scripturally that the anointing we receive can be increased. The principles for increasing the believer's anointing are the same as for the ministerial and corporate anointing.

This aspect of our spiritual walk, that we can grow in the things of the Word and the Spirit, is personally for me one that I have a deep desire to pursue. And the more I do, the hungrier I get. I often walk away from times in His Presence feeling both full and hungry. Full because He satisfies every time, hungry because I know that there is more of Him and more for me.

The Spirit spoke to me once, "You never crave for what you have never tasted."

I had never seen it that way before. But with our natural appetites, say chocolate for example—you would never have a craving for it unless you had, sometime in the past, tasted chocolate. It's the same with the things of God; the more you taste of His Presence and goodness, the more you will crave to taste them again and again.

There is a comprehensible side to the things of the Spirit that can move from beyond knowing to experiencing. I have come to understand it as a cycle. The more I know, the more I experience, and the more I experience, the more I want to know! Growth in the things of the Spirit is not measured in years as a believer, years in ministry, or even what has been accomplished for God. *Growth in God is measured by how much we know Him!*

If our hearts are right when we study and chase after the anointing, we are really studying and chasing after Him. That is where the power really is—in knowing Him.

You Have His Anointing

All that happened in the Old Testament were types and shadows to point us to Jesus and to be fulfilled in the New Testament. Contrasting with the Old Testament, we have, in the New Testament, a prophetic, royal, and priestly anointing on us.

The prophetic anointing carries supernatural wisdom and insight. The promptings of the Spirit enter your spirit through the Holy Spirit and that is how we receive knowledge and wisdom, which we would not have had otherwise.

The kingly anointing gives us supernatural power and strength. This is the anointing that gives us the ability to do the works of Jesus on the earth.

The priestly anointing brings the supernatural, divine Presence. Under the Old Covenant, God's Presence manifested as a pillar of fire and a pillar of cloud. This same Presence is now within each and every believer!

He Wants You

The reason the anointing is available to us is simply because He has plans for us. For us to do what He wants requires the anointing. So in a real way, God is both the source and the supply of our life! When God wants to speak to us, He speaks primarily to us, not to someone else. God does this because He wants you and no one else to do what He tells you. When Mary received revelation from Gabriel about God's plan for her life, she took it by faith even though she did not fully understand how it would happen. She did not immediately rush off to consult with everyone about what she had heard. Instead, she kept everything she had heard in her heart. This is how we should receive and nurture the things we hear from God about what we are to do for Him. God's word will bear fruit when it is kept in our noble and good hearts (Luke 8:15). We need to develop an attitude of discreet silence and contemplation with the things God tells us. Blaring what God tells us prematurely is a sure way to nullify the plans of God for us. *His plans for us are spoken and nurtured in intimacy.* A sign of our growth in Him is that we will love the corporate Body of Christ but we will crave intimacy with Him above all else. Our growth in Him can be measured by the amount of time we spend and continue to want to be in His Presence.

CHAPTER 8

REVERENCE AND OBEDIENCE: KEYS TO THE TANGIBLE ANOINTING

Train Your Senses

But solid food belongs to those who are of full age, that is, those who by reason of use have their senses exercised to discern both good and evil (Hebrews 5:14).

In my travels, it is common to hear believers talk about the anointing and wanting more of it. What is not as common is to hear believers talking about wanting to be trained in the anointing. For too many, the anointing remains a mysterious occurrence that happens haphazardly. Of course, if this were true then there would also be no way we could ever be trained and grow in the anointing, because how could you ever train in something that mysteriously happens without you ever knowing when, if, and how it occurs?

The anointing is heaven tangibility manifest on the earth. To be tangible means there is a physical, corporeal aspect to it. While the anointing originates as a spiritual substance, it translates to the earth realm to affect us practically and physically. Since the earth realm is physical in nature, this would also mean that to affect the earth realm and us in it the anointing would have to manifest physically.

No one is ever born "full age." Full age implies growth from a previous state of being that was not full! So we can move from "not full" to full age with the things of God! The definition of full age is that *"those who by reason of use have their senses exercised to discern both good and evil."* So the scriptural proof of a mature believer is someone who has been exercising their natural and spiritual senses to the point where they can know the difference between good and bad by God's definition. I sometimes meet believers who have an attitude of only wanting to see the good and positive in everything. It is not wrong to have a positive outlook in life and to think positively about other people, but maturing in God demands that we not just see the right and good but also the things and situations that are not right and good. Once when I was teaching this, someone came up to me after and almost berated me, saying that it was wrong to judge. I replied that it is wrong to judge people's hearts because I cannot know their hearts and I cannot always tell if they have repented, but it is always right and necessary to judge situations. We have to have our senses trained to discern and judge situations, not people.

Then there have been others I have met who only seem to discern evil and demons in everything and everyone! That's not balanced either! There is more good and more of God on the earth than there is evil! There are more angels than there are demons! It is decidedly *not* a sign of spiritual maturity to only see demons and evil everywhere!

One way that the Lord taught me to have my senses trained is to recognize the power of two simple words: *yes* and *no*. The Spirit said to me once, "*Yes* and *no* are the two most powerful words in the human vocabulary."

When you think about it, we are saved because we said "yes" to God's offer of Calvary. We are healed when we say "no" to the physical symptoms that are presented to us, no matter how real they seem. We serve God in our going because we said "yes" when we heard Him or were prompted a certain way. *Yes* and *no* are powerful words. They are spiritually potent words. They are words by which we define good and evil. The Spirit of God is not indecisive and wishy-washy—and neither should we be!

The Tangible Anointing

And Elisha said, "As the Lord of hosts lives, before whom I stand, surely were it not that I regard the presence of Jehoshaphat king of Judah, I would not look at you, nor see you. But now bring me a musician."

Then it happened, when the musician played, that the hand of the Lord came upon him (2 Kings 3:14-15).

The backstory to Elisha's comment in this conversation was a battle. The king of Israel, the king of Judah, and the king of Edom were marching against the king of Moab. They came to a dead end, a place where there was no water for them or their animals. It looked as though they would perish in the wilderness.

Jehoshaphat, the king of Judah, suddenly remembered Elisha the prophet. Elisha was called for. Elisha made it clear that he would not come if it had been the king of Israel, an idolater, who called. Like Elisha, it takes maturity to understand that there are qualifications to releasing and receiving the anointing. What qualifies or disqualifies a person is their heart attitude. The anointing is available *for* everyone but will not be received *by* everyone. *Being a dispenser of the anointing also requires that we be a discerner of hearts!* I have personally experienced people who appreciate and want the benefits of the anointing on my life but for all the wrong reasons! The anointing is symbolized by the holy anointing oil because it comes from the Holy Spirit. The anointing is for holy purposes. The Holy Spirit will not allow Himself to be party to an unholy venture—it would be unholy of anyone to even try enlisting Him!

After his discipleship and prophetic tutelage with Elijah, Elisha was undoubtedly called and anointed by God in the prophet's office. Yet although Elisha was called by God to be a prophet, the anointing was not yet flowing for him to function as one. *The anointing comes, as a seed, when we are first called but only flows as we go toward the call of God!* It takes maturity to recognize when the anointing is or isn't present, and it takes fortitude to not cave to the demands or expectations of others to "perform," pull, or make a word up when the anointing is not there to give one.

The desperate kings started making demands on Elisha to function in his prophetic office. This is the point at which weaker ministers would have given in to the pressure and said something "vaguely accurate," something along the lines of, "Yes, God loves you, so…as long as you pray enough, everything will be alright. If you do not pray enough then it will all fall apart," or, "God is with you. If you let Him, He'll lead you, and if you don't let Him, then He won't lead you."

See what I mean by "vaguely accurate"? Such words are vague enough to apply to anyone and scripturally correct enough to not be wrong. Too many "prophetic" words have a built-in failsafe. If what the "prophet" says happens, then you prayed enough and he was right. If what the prophet says doesn't happen, they you did not pray enough and still, he was right! With some of these "words," it's a case of "heads, they win and tails, you lose"! I understand and fully agree that many personal prophecies are conditional, meaning that there are things you may be instructed to do or not do in order for those words to come to pass. I also understand and agree that the majority of prophetic words are seen and spoken through a mirror, dimly (1 Corinthians 13:12), meaning that we *"know in part and we prophesy in part"* (1 Corinthians 13:9). Many times, a prophetic word delivers "a sentence from a paragraph." So I am not saying that in order for prophetic words to be legitimate, they must reveal a person's social security and bank account numbers, but on the other hand, prophetic words should carry enough of the anointing so there is some tangible weight of glory and of His Presence. *God expects us to expect more! There is specificity and clarity in the anointing!*

Once, while ministering in the Spirit to the congregation after a service, I was drawn to a man who had come in late to the meeting with a group of friends. They were seated together toward the back of the hall. I had him stand and started to pray over him. As I did, a prophetic word started to instructively rise for him about his future and what he was called to do. I said the phrase "why do you have to be right all the time" four to five times in succession and with intensity. I remember thinking as I uttered that phrase that it was an odd thing to say. After the service, one of the pastors who was supporting the meetings walked up to me, introduced that man, and told me he had something to tell me.

Driving up to the service that night, he told me that he missed his father who had passed a few months ago and that his father had always tried to steer him in the direction of God's plans for us life. He had always been a little wayward with the things of God. He was a little unsure of what to expect when I had him stand to pray for him, but what very suddenly caught his attention was when I started prophesying about his future and, by the Spirit, started saying some of the same things that his dad had told him. In particular, he said, "When you repeatedly said 'why do you have to be right all the time?' I started to cry hard because that's exactly what my father used to say to me, and the tone you used as you said it was exactly how he

115

would say it. It was as if I heard God speaking to me, first through my father and now through you."

Again, God expects us to expect more! There is specificity and clarity in the anointing!

I once heard the Lord say, "I'm training up marksmen in the Spirit." No one trains to remain the same. Training always implies an intention to move closer toward marksmanship.

It is right, good, and necessary to know that scripturally and spiritually, believers have the anointing, but it's another thing to have believers trained in that anointing!

Being called up by the four kings to give them a word from God, Elisha was in a situation that not only called for a prophetic anointing but for the fear of God. At this point many ministers would have desperately tried to make up with oratory skills, talents, and intellect that only the anointing could ever produce. But Elisha knew better! He knew the anointing was not present, but he also knew how to draw on the anointing.

To be trained in the anointing includes knowing what to do when the anointing is present but it also includes knowing what to do when the anointing is not present.

Reverence

When the anointing is in manifestation, our response must be obedience.

When the anointing is not in manifestation, our response must be reverence.

When the anointing is in manifestation, our response must be obedience. When the anointing is not in manifestation, our response must be reverence.

Reverence, because it is the fear of God that restrains us, so we do not act on our own accord outside of the move of the Spirit.

Reverence, because that is the posture that puts God first, gives God honor, and ushers His Presence into the room.

Reverence, because you acknowledge that without God you will not and, importantly, you cannot.

It is the respectful fear of God, a reverence for the Spirit, that is the root of us wanting to move in the Spirit *decently, in order, and accurately*.

It repudiates the authority of Holy Spirit when believers act or speak out of turn in an environment where believes gather to hear from the Holy Spirit.

I was ministering in a series of meetings a few years ago where the Spirit had been ministering beautifully to us. They had a rotation of worship leaders each night. One evening, they had a younger worship leader leading us. He was a reasonably good vocalist and musician. Toward the end of the worship segment of the service, he led us in a chorus that ushered in the Presence of God in a strong way. You could sense the glory slowly but surely descending on us thickly. Just as the congregation slowly and spontaneously started to come to a place of quiet and stillness before the Presence, the worship leader started to loudly cry over the microphone and said, "I am so thankful for this opportunity. This is a team effort. Can you all please join me in thanking the sound crew back there in the sound booth?" Everyone in the congregation turned around and started to applaud the sound crew—and immediately ushered the Presence of God right out of the building!

As good as the sound crew was and as much as they deserved to be appreciated, turning to applaud them just as we were entering into deep worship and as the Presence was settling on us was decidedly *not* the time to do that! It showed a clear lack of spiritual discernment of the moving of the Spirit and an absolute lack of reverence for the Presence of God. If I had already been handed the service, I would have stopped it. But since I had not, I did the next best thing and taught on it for a bit before I started preaching instead. Spiritually, it is never in good taste to seek to honor man in place of worshiping God! That is out of spiritual order because it clearly was not done under the leadership of the Spirit!

On another occasion, at another meeting, the anointing to prophesy swept into the room. I could sense a word from the Spirit starting to pour forth. As I made my way to the pulpit to deliver that prophetic word, someone from way at the back of the auditorium started to deliver a message in tongues, and someone else standing by him started to give the interpretation. They were so far at the back of the auditorium that really no one could hear anything intelligibly. The pastor who had the microphone and was hosting the service that night tried to tell them that no one could hear them, but they were so lost in their own world, yelling out, that they did not even hear him! Finally the ushers had to go to them and quiet them down.

There must be order in the delivery of spiritual gifts! The Spirit would not inspire a message through tongues and interpretations that no one can hear. If they did feel they had a message from God for the congregation, they should have made themselves known to the leadership and allowed the leadership to decide if they could have the microphone to deliver the message properly. After the ushers had got them to quiet down and I was given the pulpit, I was able to still my heart again and tap back into that prophetic flow to deliver that word I had originally sensed. If I had not tapped back into that flow and delivered that word, congregationally, we would all been robbed of what God wanted to say and the flow He had wanted for that service.

How Elisha Got the Anointing to Flow

Not only did Elisha know enough to sense that the anointing was not present, he evidently knew how to get it to flow. He asked for a musician. Anointed music touches a person's soul realm before it touches their spirit being. Music touches and opens a person up emotionally. This is why you see hordes of people having very wild emotional displays at concerts. As believers we have the capacity for anointed praise and worship to move us past a soul experience to a spiritual experience. Part of being skilled and trained in the anointing is demonstrating the ability to know the difference between a soul-emotional encounter and a spiritual-anointing encounter. Even though we are to *"walk by faith not by sight"* (2 Corinthians 5:7), which basically means that as believers we do not allow for our emotions to lead us, there is nothing innately wrong about having a soul-emotional encounter—unless we mistake it for a spiritual-anointing one instead! Knowing how to pierce the division between soul and spirit requires wielding the double-edged sword of the Spirit (Hebrews 4:12). It takes a good grasp of the Word to know if our soul or our spirit is speaking!

The right music can open our hearts to the flow of the Spirit!

Elijah had heard directly from God that Elisha was called to be a prophet and was to be his successor. Yet Elisha took about ten years as he waited on God and served Elijah. Serving Elijah up close, he had the opportunity to observe Elijah closely and see how skillful he was with the anointing. Elisha knew that it was the anointing that made Elijah the man he was. By the time Elijah was going to be caught up to heaven, Elisha had followed the prompting of the Spirit in asking for a double portion of the anointing. Elisha would have had no other reason to ask and expect that he could receive this. Elijah tested Elisha's hunger for the double portion anointing four times.

When Elijah asked him what he wanted, Elisha did not need to think it over for a day or two. A double portion of Elijah's anointing was the object of his quest. As the chariots of fire came to take Elijah, Elisha saw and cried after him. Elijah dropped his mantle—a symbol of the anointing—and Elisha took it and wore it (2 Kings 2:13).

Elisha had persistence and determination to enter into all that God had for him!

Elisha had to learn the tangibility of the anointing. He had to distinguish his natural feelings from the supernatural senses of the manifested anointing upon his body. Through time, experience, and Elijah's tutelage, he learned the difference between the anointing in manifestation and the anointing in latency, and so the tangibility of the anointing increased upon his life.

Jesus Flowed in a Tangible Anointing

And Jesus, immediately knowing in Himself that power had gone out of Him, turned around in the crowd and said, "Who touched My clothes?" (Mark 5:30)

The only two people who knew that "power had gone out of Him" were the lady who got healed and Jesus. It was not obvious to any-one else. Faith activated the anointing in Jesus, and faith caused the lady to be receptively open to the flow. So we can see that *faith causes the flow of the anointing!* Faith is actually how everything we receive from God flows. Jesus was not even aware of or focused on this lady when she got healed. Just as she drew the anointing by her faith, we can draw the anointing by our faith! There had to be others around her and Jesus who had ailments. There had to be others who had touched Jesus. The disciples themselves said, when Jesus asked who touched Him, that the multitudes were thronging Him (Mark 5:31). This means that the crowd was jostling around Jesus as He made His way to Jairus' house. But it was only the touch of faith that drew the anointing! The others who touched Jesus out of curiosity did not receive anything.

The anointing, released and received by faith, produces tangible results in the physical, natural realm. However euphoric, the tangibility of the anointing goes beyond just feelings and emotions. But there is also a side of the anointing that is tangible enough that it can be felt in our bodies and our emotions. This is why our minds need to be renewed with the Word, so that our emotions are tapered into unison with our spirits. Sensing the anointing is not being led by our emotions. The former comes from a place of deep knowing, responding to the prompting and drawing of the Spirit; the latter is flighty and based on our likes, dislikes, and our self-imposed, preconceived ideas.

Whenever I have led services where there has been a flow of the Spirit with a tangible anointing, I have always encouraged the congregation to do two things. First, I tell them to yield to whatever they sense the anointing is leading them to—to "give in" to the nudging of the Spirit. This might mean they cry, they laugh, they shake, or they fall over. Or it might mean they fall on their face in worship. It might mean they run around the room. It could mean any number of things to any number of people! Part of our training in sensitivity to the anointing is to not be held back by what we think other people are thinking of us. The power in the anointing is released as we no longer care what other people think of us! As long as we are bound by a "what will they think" mentality, we will never dare step out of the boat like Peter did (Matthew 14:28-29)! It takes boldness to follow after the anointing!

A pastor asked me once, after attending such a service, how I knew that everyone who responded was responding in the Spirit and not in the flesh. I asked him how he knew, on a Sunday morning when he was having his regular services, if all his congregation was in the Spirit as they were listening to him preach or if any of them were in the flesh. I asked him if he ever stopped the service because a few people were thinking about where to go for lunch after church instead of concentrating on the sermon he was ministering. We do not stop a service because some are not hungry or are acting in the flesh. We continue allowing for the flow of the Spirit to cater to those who are hungry! Those who are not hungry should not dictate how those who are hungry feast at the Father's table!

The other thing I tell people at these services that I am leading is to be aware how the room senses to them. The anointing can be sensed. I used the word *sense* purposely to differentiate from the word *feel*. In this context, I use *sense* as a spiritual sensation and *feel* as an emotional sensation. While it is not wrong to have emotions, since God gave us the ability to have them, it is wrong to be led by them and use them as the measuring stick for our life because emotions are very much subject to our external stimuli, which is changeable and may likely be contradictory to the Word of God.

One way we can learn how to anticipate and cooperate with the flow of the anointing is by being attentive whenever we are in the room where the anointing is flowing. We can learn how to sense the anointing so that we will recognize it the next time it starts to flow.

When the Lord first started having me call out specific physical ailments while I was preaching, so that the healing flow would touch people, I would sense a warmth on parts of my own body. As I would focus in on that warmth, the Spirit would reveal specifics about what He was wanting to heal. I also found that when I did call those ailments out from the pulpit, that same warmth would be felt by the people responding to that call on the parts of their body that needed a healing touch. So I've learned to cooperate when I sense the warm heat of the anointing.

Another way I will many times sense the anointing is like a wave. The sense I get is like I am standing on a beach and strong waves come rolling in, sweeping over me. I have had this sense of "waves" first roll toward me then roll out from me, and I have seen people healed and delivered from it.

To be sent like Jesus was sent includes learning the flow of the anointing. It is part and parcel of being a disciple of Jesus Christ and being an effective witness!

THE ANOINTING TO GATHER AND GOVERN

CHAPTER 9

JESUS BUILDS HIS CHURCH

The outpouring of the Spirit on the day of Pentecost and the accompanying anointing of His Presence on the sons and daughters of God did not just signify the ministry of the Holy Spirit on the earth, but it also allowed for the continuation of the ministry of Jesus through His Church.

Although the anointing's operation in the life of a believer—to lead us to grow in our walk with God and go into all the world—occurs concurrently and unceasingly, there is systematic function to the anointing. *The more we grow, the further we can go!* Even after we start going, we will continue to need the anointing to teach and lead us into growth. *A disciple cannot make disciples if he is not being discipled himself!*

The plan of God for our growth is that He can send us forth to represent Him as sons and daughters. And God wants to send us forth so that we can reclaim the earth back to God's original purpose for it! Part of God's purpose for the creation of man was that He might, through them, bring forth revelation and understanding of His nature and character. The light of this revelation that God would utter forth through man would then dispel the darkness that satan had sought to enslave mankind with. God ordained that man should "*not live by bread alone, but by every word that proceeds from the mouth of God*" (Matthew 4:4). In other words, God's ideal was that man live by communicative revelation.

The process by which revelation is brought forth on the earth is through the vehicle of the anointing manifesting through sons and daughters of God speaking and acting under the inspiration of the Spirit.

The anointing does not just displace darkness but more importantly also establishes righteousness! The anointing seeks to establish the rule of God on the earth realm.

If the systems of the kingdom of darkness were displaced but nothing was established in its place, in that void, chaos would soon ensue again. Jesus summed it up in Matthew 12:43-45 this way:

> *When an unclean spirit goes out of a man, he goes through dry places, seeking rest, and finds none. Then he says, "I will return to my house from which I came." And when he comes, he finds it empty, swept, and put in order. Then he goes and takes with him seven other spirits more wicked than himself, and they enter and dwell there; and the last state of that man is worse than the first. So shall it also be with this wicked generation.*

So, spiritually and then naturally, we should not just look to "tear down" the works of the enemy but also, actively, toward the building up of the things of God. The same anointing that destroys the work of the enemy is also able to build the house of God!

I have seen some believers and ministers overcommit to discerning and casting out demons from places and people. I say "overcommit" because it seems that is all they do and are concerned about. While we should *always* want the oppressed to be set free, we should be equally concerned, or perhaps even more so, about making sure they are built and filled up with the Word and the Spirit *after* they are set free. Too many times, altars are filled with the same believers seeking deliverance, week after week. For many of these believers, they do not just need to be set free, but what they need is to be taught to stay free!

Setting captives free *alone* does not build the Kingdom! The Kingdom is built when believers are developed and walk in their callings as ordained by God. If we tear down without rebuilding, then all we will have is the inhabitable ruins of the previous structure!

Jesus' Building Project

*And I also say to you that you are Peter, and on this rock **I will build My church**, and the gates of Hades shall not prevail against it. And I will give you the keys of the kingdom of heaven, and whatever you bind on earth will be bound in heaven, and whatever you loose on earth will be loosed in heaven* (Matthew 16:18-19).

Revelation, a divine enlightening of our natural and spiritual understanding, is what we experience when we receive communication from God. Establishing and building the Church through men who have received revelation is the means by which God manifests on the earth realm.

The life and ministry of Jesus continues today through each and every disciple as they function under the anointing. The Church is comprised of disciples, the living stones, and the spiritual and theological fabric of the seen and the unseen Body. Building the Body of Christ lies with the five specific ministry manifestations of the Messiah listed in Ephesians 4:11—apostles, prophets, evangelists, pastors, and teachers.

When taken together in their complete function, these five ministerial offices express the ministry of Christ as seen in the Gospels, amplified in the Epistles, and experienced today throughout the Body of Christ.

Jesus is our Chief Apostle (Hebrews 3:1), Prophet (Mark 6:4; Luke 13:33), Evangelist (Luke 4:18; Matthew 18:11), Pastor (John 10:11;

Hebrews 13:20), and Teacher (Matthew 23:10). These same five ministerial functions that Jesus personified completely are offices that God calls and sets different disciples in. It takes all of us in the Body to add up to One of Him!

The governance of Jesus over the Church is exercised through these specific ministries of Jesus manifested through those called and walking in the five-fold ministry offices.

In governing, we will see later on that the ministry offices do not rule over the Church, but rather they nourish and administer the word and will of the Lord to the Body, and in doing so, provide divine order for God's people.

Every minister called to any of these offices functions at various lesser degrees of the anointing than Jesus did. So not a single apostle, prophet, evangelist, pastor, or teacher ministering today operates in the same full measure of the anointing that Jesus did. *They partake in a measure of the full measure of Christ.*

These five-fold office anointings are functioning, practical operations and not just fancy titles! I have met people who handed me their business cards calling themselves "apostle" or "prophet" only to find out they hardly went anywhere to preach nor did they have a track record of having established anything of ministerial substance. We need to acknowledge and honor these anointings by recognizing them, and the way we do recognize them is by the actual fruit they produce. *Fruit is always a manifestation of the root!*

I have spoken to individuals who have a true call to one of these five offices, but because they have not yet developed into that office and anointing, I cautioned them against announcing their ministry with titles before they bear fruit.

The intent of God in anointing us to grow and then sending us out with the anointing is far beyond our personal development. The anointing is ultimately for the building of the Body of Christ, the Church, which in turn is the vessel by which the world will be reached with the love of God. So in His plans to build the Church, Jesus, as the main Architect, employs and oversees a host of "contractors"—ministerial workers who facilitate the implementing of His master blueprints.

Just as God's plan for man is that they be cleansed by the Blood and filled with the Spirit, God's plan for the earth is that it be redeemed from the curse and functioning under the reign of Heaven.

The anointing to gather and govern, which is bringing divine order into the earth realm, must first be exercised in the Church. As a consequence of applying the anointing in faith and exercising the authority given to the Church, it will spread to regions and people groups.

On a personal level, whenever the Gospel is preached and someone turns to Christ, divine order and governance has made its way into that person.

When a believer stands in faith and receives answered prayer, that is a result of the governance of Heaven overriding what would otherwise be a natural course of events.

In calming the storm, raising the dead, and multiplying food for the masses, Jesus was exercising the governance of heaven over the restrictions and disruptions of the natural realm.

The gathering of the people of God under the governance of God on the earth is what happens when it is "*on earth as it is in heaven*" (Matthew 6:10)!

God's Original Command

Then God blessed them and said, "Be fruitful and multiply. Fill the earth and govern it. Reign over the fish in the sea, the birds in the sky, and all the animals that scurry along the ground" (Genesis 1:28 NLT).

Now, we see that God's original instruction to Adam and Eve was actually the governance of the earth. Because of their transgression and sin that then entered the human race, governance of the earth, having the ways of heaven on the earth, involves and requires that individuals come under the governance of God's Spirit so that, through them, ultimately society can be influenced by those believers.

To be clear, scripture does not advocate for the Church to stage a political or military coup in every country so it can be "Christian territory."

All through the New Testament writings, we see that the early Church did not pray or plot to overthrow the Romans so that there would be a Christianized Rome. History has shown the fallacy of this ideology whenever it has been attempted. Emperor Constantine proved this when in A.D. 312 he claimed to have a vision of a sign in the sky and converted to Christianity. He legalized Christianity and then sought to enforce it on everyone else. Since it was now socially beneficial to be a Christian, people no longer became Christians out of a heart conviction. The distinction between the Church and the world was blurred, and the result was the Church became worldly. This ultimately paved the way for the medieval Dark Ages in which major segments of those claiming to be the Church were openly corrupt and drunk with the power of their own political clout.

However, the flip side is also equally true—believers, led and anointed by the Spirit, should exercise their rights and be actively involved in all political and social processes available to them, not to enforce their theology on the ideology of society but to ensure that the Church be free to proclaim throughout society what the Word and the Spirit are saying. Political offices seek to legislate the actions of society without speaking to the nature of their heart, but the true Church is after the hearts of people. Obviously, a right heart will lead to right actions, but legalized actions don't always come from right hearts. As with any arena in life for the believer, it takes the call of God and the anointing of the Spirit to be involved in the political landscape of any nation—and as with Adam and Eve, God's heart is that His reign would extend through the hearts of individuals to their immediate surroundings, their own gardens of Eden!

> *Satan, who is the god of this world, has blinded the minds of those who don't believe. They are unable to see the glorious light of the Good News. They don't understand this message about the glory of Christ, who is the exact likeness of God* (2 Corinthians 4:4 NLT).

The anointing to govern was God's ultimate plan for man from the beginning. God was not just looking to redeem His creation, man, but also the garden God had placed man in! We understand that God is not just concerned about real estate, but He is concerned about the inhabitants of the land!

The anointing for the conquest of regions is not for conquering people but for holding back demonic forces so that everyone can hear the Word of the Lord unhindered.

The anointing to govern holds back the darkness first so that people can see the light and then, second, keeps the darkness at bay so that the believers who have seen the light can be developed in the ways of the light!

For too long churches have had a "win them and leave them" mentality with evangelism and missions. But the governing anointing on the five ministry gifts of Jesus don't want to just win them and leave them. These ministry specialists want to win them and build them!

A building is a structure that stands and has some tangible permanence. This is so with natural, physical buildings but is also true of the spiritual building, the Church that Jesus is building! Success in ministry is not just in how many respond to an altar call to receive Jesus but also in how many continue in the Way and are discipled into maturity.

God's Goal: Disciples

Then the eleven disciples went away into Galilee, to the mountain which Jesus had appointed for them. When they saw Him, they worshiped Him; but some doubted.

And Jesus came and spoke to them, saying, "All authority has been given to Me in heaven and on earth. Go therefore and make disciples of all the nations, baptizing them in the name of the Father and of the Son and of the Holy Spirit, teaching them to observe all things that I have commanded you; and lo, I am with you always, even to the end of the age." Amen (Matthew 28:16-20).

The ministerial anointing gathers us, calling us away from the worldly, humanistic system and puts us under the governance of God's divine order.

A short few years after I had first started in ministry, without any intentional planning on my part, I started having pastors and ministers gather around me and allow me a voice in their lives and ministry. I did not know then what I know now about the anointing. I did not recognize that one aspect of the call of God on my life would be that I would have a part in leaders being raised up and gathered. Because I was newer in ministry and, in some cases, younger than some of the leaders, I started thinking that there was something more I needed to walk in for this position of promotion that I had found myself in. I went before the Lord in a season of prayer to seek Him. After a few days, I had an encounter with the Lord that has changed my outlook of ministry to this day.

In that visitation, one of the things that the Lord pointed out to me was that the command in Matthew 28 was to go forth and make disciples, but I had been more concerned about making converts! The Lord then said to me, "There is no discipleship without relationship!" I instantly understood that I had inadvertently been in a hurry to get the altars filled and the people saved, but then I was in an equal hurry to move back home or on to the next series of meetings. God helped me see that my call, and really the call on the Church, was to make disciples and not just converts. I immediately changed the way I approached those ministers who had gathered around me. Instead of just meeting them to organize and plan the next conference or project, I started intentionally spending time with each of them, sharing my heart, and hearing theirs, talking about what the Lord was teaching me and growing me into.

Shortly after, I preached an evangelistic meeting and felt led to gather those who had responded in those meetings into a congregation because that area did not have a Spirit-filled one. I installed a couple whom I had been spending time with as the pastors. That small group of new believers grew and flourished as a church, and for many years after we conducted many missions outreaches using it as a base. It wasn't long before I duplicated this in many other places and saw other churches and ministries raised up! God had shown me a blueprint for building!

Although this verse in Matthew is rightly recognized as the Great Commission of the Church that commissions *all* believers, in its context Jesus was actually not speaking to His main body of followers but His eleven original disciples who would be the initial apostles of the Church.

I am not in any way suggesting that the Great Commission only applied to the original eleven apostles or that it only applies today to those in the five-fold ministry. But like with everything else that God does, there is divine order and divine specificity. Order, because foundations have to be laid before the building can be erected. Specificity, because the anointing empowers through calling, practice in yielding to the Spirit, and maturity in God. So the Spirit does not anoint you to be a plumber if God has called you to be a carpenter!

The original eleven disciples were sent forth to "make disciples," baptizing them to announce their new birth in Christ, and then teaching them. So we see that Jesus' order, as they were sent, was to make disciples by preaching salvation and then teaching.

The Church is established by both the preaching and the teaching of the Gospel! Jesus Christ is not just to be preached about, but He is also to be taught about!

The anointing to govern the Church, by the demonstrative preaching, teaching, and living of Jesus' life and message, fell on the initial eleven apostles, who in turn are examples for those called into the five-fold ministry today.

Specialized Laborers

And He Himself gave some to be apostles, some prophets, some evangelists, and some pastors and teachers, for the equipping of the saints for the work of ministry, for the edifying of the body of Christ, till we all come to the unity of the faith and of the knowledge of the Son of God, to a perfect man, to the measure of the stature of the fullness of Christ; that we should no longer be children, tossed to and fro and carried about with every wind of doctrine, by the trickery of men, in the cunning craftiness of deceitful plotting, but, speaking the truth in love, may grow up in all things into Him who is the head—Christ—from whom the whole body, joined and knit together by what every joint supplies, according to the effective working by which every part does its share, causes growth of the body for the edifying of itself in love (Ephesians 4:11–16).

Preaching, teaching, and living the life and ministry of Jesus is not the role of the five-fold ministers alone. It is simply their place, by the call of God, to teach and train others in the Body to go teach and train others!

On one side of the ditch, some have completely ignored these five ministry offices, especially that of the apostle and prophet, saying these ended with the early Church. On the other side of the ditch, some have over-exalted these five ministry offices—again, especially that of the apostle and the prophet. But as with all matters, it is the balanced middle path that will lead to stability and longevity. These are five specific callings and anointings that God has ordained to lead His Body. They are not better than but they are different in function from the rest of the Body. We do need to recognize and honor these anointings to receive from them, but we also need to recognize that it is the grace of God through them and in them from God for us! God as the Source did not call and anoint them so that they can be elevated among us but that they could be additional vessels through whom God could mature us. They lay the structural framework that the house is then built and dressed upon.

God the Father, in His wisdom and mercy, does not will to have men and women born again and then turned loose, armed with just the Bible and the Holy Spirit! Like any other relationship, our relationship with the Word and the Spirit of God require time and guidance to develop. Just as we would not give our car keys to a five-year-old to drive with, God treasures us too much to just leave us alone to our devices to develop spiritually. He set forth the ministry gifts to assist in the governing of our growth and the development of the house of God.

The five ministry gift offices are leadership callings. This does not just mean titled, positional leadership but morally influential leadership. This requires that they have a voice to others and a platform from which to influence others.

These five anointings, in all their different forms, are vital to the Body. Paul laid out in Ephesians 4 that when in operation, these ministry anointings serve the Body by:

- equipping the saints for the work of the ministry
- edifying the Body of Christ
- bringing us toward the unity of the faith, a knowledge of the Son of God
- growing us to maturity, to a perfect man
- bringing us to the measure of the stature of the fullness of Christ
- stabilizing us so that we not be as children, tossed to and fro

The opposite must then be true. When we don't see the Body nourished and flourishing, it is a clear sign of the absence of these anointings. The result is that the Body will be scattered and lawless by God's standards.

Each of these five office functions of the anointing gather the Body of Christ so it can be nourished and empowered with the reality of our rights in Christ.

It never fails to escape me that Paul, in writing here to the Ephesian church, warned them against being children, with the possibility of their being *tossed to and fro and carried about with every wind of doctrine*. What could possibly toss them about was not persecution, lack, sickness, or even demonic attacks but simply doctrinal instability. This cues me in to the importance of doctrine or teaching. If even the Ephesian church with all her access to the earliest believers and apostles was in danger of being tossed about by the "cunning craft-iness of man," then how much more do we need to be on guard today? The establishment of proper fundamental doctrines is the pil-lar on which we, the house of God, stand. This is where the five-fold minister's anointed abilities to gather and govern are vital to the growth and stability of the Body.

How urgently we need these anointings in operation today! The modern Church has been able to gather crowds the size of which was unheard of in previous generations. More than ever, we need to allow for the anointing not just to gather the crowds but also to bring the government of God into our midst!

CHAPTER 10

ASSORTED ANOINTINGS ON ASSIGNMENT

Just as our hands have five fingers, so the hand of God, working in and on the Church, has five fingers. And just as our whole body would lack if we were missing any one finger or thumb, so also does the Body of Christ suffer if we lack any one of these ministries.

These five main ministries of the Church balance each other out. Flowing together, they balance the Body of Christ.

In studying these anointings individually, it would help us to remember that not everyone is called to one of these offices. So everyone is not an apostle or a prophet or one of the other ministry offices. But in a very real sense, everyone in the Body of Christ has access to a touch of that anointing on them. This is because as believers, we have the Holy Spirit living on the inside of us and the Holy Spirit is the Source of all of those anointings. It was the Spirit, as the Source of these anointings, that came upon Jesus and endued Him to walk in these offices as a Man anointed by the Spirit in the earth realm. Just like Jesus, the Holy Spirit is also apostolically sent, prophetically profound, evangelistically compassionate, pastorally protective, and apt to teach deep truths simply.

Again, we can see that there are two ditches we want to avoid with this. On one side of the ditch is the idea that everyone is an apostle, a prophet, or one of the other gifts. One the other side is the idea that no one ever qualifies in our day. As always, it's the middle path that is balanced and accurate. Everyone is not called to one of these five ministry offices. Yet all of these five callings are available today. This is made very clear in Ephesians 4:13:

> *Till we all come to the unity of the faith and of the knowledge of the Son of God, to a perfect man, to the measure of the stature of the fullness of Christ.*

Everyone would agree that the Body of Christ has not reached the unity of the faith, nor have we reached *"a perfect man...of the stature of the fullness of Christ."* This then necessitates the continuation of these ministries among us.

In a circular fashion, the anointing to grow and the anointing to go leads to the anointing to gather and govern, which in turn fuels the anointing to grow and go.

All three functions of the anointing we have looked at in this book have the same Source, flow through the same vessels, and bring us to the same destination. The Source, of course, is the Holy Spirit; the vessels, the members of the Body of Christ; and the destination, the establishment of the plans of God toward seeking and saving that which was lost!

The ministry gifts gather, nourish, and lead the believers to grow spiritually and then to go into all their world. As they do, some will hear the call and walk into one of the five ministry offices.

There is unity in diversity in the things of the Spirit! Each aspect of the anointing complements all the other aspects of the anointing. As believers, we get to feast on the spread that the Spirit lays before us!

These five ministry offices are diverse and operate in seemingly different ways. Even within each of the five offices, there is a diversity of how the anointing manifests. So every pastor, for example, will not have the same emphasis, leadership, and delivery styles or even ministry and church goals. It helps us to recognize not just the ministry office but the particular flow and emphasis that each minister walks in. We receive better when we know what to believe for from each minister from whom we draw.

Because they are the most commonly accepted throughout the Church world, we will take a short look at the office of the teacher, pastor, and evangelist in this chapter and spend a little more time on the apostle and the prophet in the next.

The Teacher

The ministry of the teacher and teaching is found all through the New Testament. The Epistles were all teaching-based letters circulating through the early Church. They were written either to correct or to clarify issues that churches faced. In the Gospels, we see Jesus the Teacher; in the Epistles, we see the Holy Spirit continuing to teach through the ministry of the apostles.

The function of teaching is so important that it is the only one of the five offices that is listed in all three passages of scripture that we have looked at where Paul mentions groupings of giftings. So teaching is needed in our growing (Romans 12:4-8), in our going (1 Corinthians 12:4-8), and in our gathering and governing (Ephesians 4:11)!

Another interesting thing that we will see as we study these five governing offices is that seldom does a minister strictly flow just in one office.

> *Now in the church that was at Antioch there were certain prophets and teachers: Barnabas, Simeon who was called Niger, Lucius of Cyrene, Manaen who had been brought up with Herod the tetrarch, and Saul* (Acts 13:1).

Earlier on in Acts 11:22-26, Barnabas was identified as a teacher, but we now see him here listed as a prophet and teacher. Elsewhere, Paul himself was also named a prophet and teacher (Galatians 1:12; Ephesians 3:3; 1 Timothy 2:7), and later on in Acts 14:14 we see both Paul and Barnabas named apostles!

As we saw in Section 1 of this book with the growing anointing gifts in Romans 12 and in Section 2 with the going anointing gifts in 1 Corinthians 12, the gathering and governing anointing gifts here in Ephesians 4 flow seamlessly with and through each other. They are all distinct by definition but also have a semblance of similitude in function so that the lines of distinction are not always easy to see.

Many times, while I am teaching or preaching, there will come a flow of prophecy or a word of knowledge that almost seems like it's a part of the message. It brought a prophetic flow into the service that added to the teaching of the Word. This is another reason why it's important for ministers not to be so tied to our notes and outlines that we shut off the flow of the Spirit! Healings, deliverances, and salvations can happen even when there is a teacher teaching a Bible study! While those may be more prominent in the evangelist office, for example, we should not place limits on what the Spirit can do in any meeting!

All these five gathering and governing anointings are divine empowerments and not just natural abilities alone. So someone called to be a teacher isn't just someone who knows a lot about the Bible. For sure, a Bible teacher should be knowledgeable of the Bible, but what qualifies them is the manifest anointing to illuminate not just the minds but the hearts of their hearers. Teachers teach the Word in a way that makes it comes alive and, importantly, attainable. Faith is always the result of hearing those called to this office, because teachers teach the Word and faith always comes when we hear the Word (Romans 10:17).

I planted, Apollos watered, but God gave the increase. So then
neither he who plants is anything, nor he who waters, but God who
gives the increase. Now he who plants and he who waters are one,
and each one will receive his own reward according to his own labor
(1 Corinthians 3:6-8).

Here, Paul called teaching "watering." Watering is a process necessary after seeds have been deposited in the ground to activate life and
growth to the seed. Planting without watering endangers the growth
of the seed. God's order is first that seeds be planted, then to water the
seed, and then growth or increase comes. This means that for all of us
who have had the initial seed of the Gospel planted in us, it is crucial
that we get under good "watering" so that God can cause increase
from that seed to spring forth in our life.

Doctors use the term *failure to thrive* when infants are not growing
as expected. It is usually a sign that the child is undernourished. I
have met believers who are born again and Spirit filled and still fail
to thrive, and the reasons are the same as those children—they're
malnourished! We will always need to be reminded that Jesus died
for us, but we also need to know *why* He did and *how* we can appropriate what He purchased for us! This is what teachers do—they
show us what all else, besides a heavenly mansion, is ours because
of Jesus' sacrifice! Teachers establish us in who we are in Christ, our
benefits, and our proper responses to the things of the Word and the
Spirit.

Apollos, as a teacher who came watering after Paul planted the
Corinthian church, had a reputation of being much help to believers
(Acts 18:27). Many believers need the "much help" that can only
come from the teaching ministry. I have seen the need of this firsthand. Any evangelistic effort is incomplete without incorporating the
follow-up of the pastoral and teaching offices!

This is true for everyone, but I have seen the extreme of this in many third-world countries. Statistically, after the altars are flooded or an ocean of hands are raised to receive Jesus, not much else changes in that community unless there are local churches involved or raised up from those evangelistic meetings. This is the apostolic blueprint for taking regions for God! Teachers and pastors partake of the evangelist's harvest of wheat and work it into being flour and ultimately bread that can then be tasted by all. God's plan is that the harvest be brought into the storehouse, not left to rot in the fields!

The anointing gathers us so that the anointing can govern us!

> *The anointing gathers us so that the anointing can govern us!*

I have noticed that some teachers seem to be given a topical emphasis, like faith or healing, from the Spirit to bring to the Body, while others simply and powerfully teach the text and the context of the Bible itself. Then, there are some who are not thought of as teachers in the traditional sense but are set by God to teach by demonstrating the flow of the Spirit and the anointing. *By precept and by example, the Holy Spirit aims to teach us the ways of God!*

The Pastor

While the word *pastor* is only used once in the King James Version, here in Ephesians 4:11, there are many references to the role and function of this, perhaps the most visible and widely accepted of the five offices.

Pastor, from the Greek *poimen*, actually means "shepherd" and is translated 17 times in the New Testament as such. Only once is it translated "pastor." The shepherd is one who tends the herd and flock, guiding as well as feeding.

The shepherds function as overseers (Acts 20:28), from the Greek *episkopos,* which is also translated "bishop" in other places (see Philippians 1:1; 1 Timothy 3:2; Titus 1:7; 1 Peter 2:25).

We can easily see that Jesus is the Great Shepherd, the Chief Shepherd. Jesus modeled in perfection the function of the Overseer of our soul.

The pastor is dear to the heart of God in that, of the five ministry anointings, the pastor spends the most time among the sheep. Sheep have a dependance on their shepherd for their survival. It is important that we see the symbolism of God referring to Himself and Jesus as the Shepherd and us as His sheep. Sheep need to be led to feed and to have shelter. Sheep have no resources and are defenseless otherwise. So the relationship between sheep and shepherd is really one of the sheep's wellbeing.

This is the responsibility that those called to pastor today walk in. As under-shepherds to the Head Shepherd, pastors have the anointing-given ability to lead God's flock as God Himself intends.

Having pastored myself, I always endeavored to remember that inasmuch as I was anointed to pastor the flock, I was also answerable to the Head Shepherd for the care I afforded them. In the natural, if we left our children to the care of a nanny or a tutor, we would expect a certain level of care to be provided for our children. We would rightly expect it, and the caregiver would be obliged to provide it. Our heavenly Father is no different when He places His children under the care of His under-shepherds. In the local church, from those who are spiritually newborn to the adolescents and then the grownups, the under-shepherd is equipped by the anointing to provide the sustenance required for their wellbeing. *The Father's nurturing is expressed in and through the pastoral anointing.*

Like a mother hen who protectively gathers her chicks, so the pastoral anointing is well able to gather the children of God in a family-like setting. That is the essence of the local church.

And when he brings out his own sheep, he goes before them; and the sheep follow him, for they know his voice (John 10:4).

This refers to Jesus the Head Shepherd but applies to all His under-shepherds as well. Pastors then must be leaders of the flock and not the other way around. There is a gentle strength that accompanies the pastoral anointing—gentle enough to care for the weakest of lambs yet, like David, strong enough to fight off the lion and the bear when necessary.

Like all the other five ministry gifts, pastoring is essentially a calling and a vocation that must be God-called and recognized by man but not man-appointed.

The flavor of a local church is often characteristic of the pastor himself. He sets the tone. A prayerful pastor will produce a prayerful congregation. If missions is on the pastor's heart, then the church will have a missions emphasis. Just as Jesus is the Gate to the sheepfold of salvation, the pastor is the gate to the culture of the local church.

God will plant us in a church that has an emphasis and flow that will cultivate our individual call! The local church we are connected to both nourishes our call and draws it out of us. After I got born again, the first church I attended had a very strong missions outreach. It was almost all they talked about every week. It was only years after, when I was already active in ministry and missions, that I understood what an impact and impartation they had made in me. *The anointing operates on a deep calling to deep (Psalm 42:2) principle. So the anointing on my life calls out to anointings around me that are necessary to mature it. And the anointings around me draw out from me the anointings I have yet to know about! The anointing stirs and deposits!*

When the Spirit plants believers in a local church, it's not so they can just be members there. The Spirit intends that they be partakers of the anointing on that house! It is not an issue of membership; it is an issue of impartation!

> *And I will give you shepherds according to My heart, who will feed*
> *you with knowledge and understanding* (Jeremiah 3:15).

The pastor doesn't just lead but he also facilitates with the feeding of the flock. This means that either the pastor is able to effectively teach the Word or else ensure that there are others on the regular schedule of the church who can. Not only must the feeding of the Word be regular but the feeding must be balanced. This means that no church should overemphasize its emphasis!

> *But we will give ourselves continually to prayer and to the ministry*
> *of the word* (Acts 6:4).

One of the best things anyone called to pastoring can do to step into their call is to develop a love for the Word and a spirit of prayer. This was what the early church leaders chose to do over the practical demands of the growing congregation. They realized that as ministers if they did not tend to their own inner life, they would be of no effect to those around them. This is still true today!

The Evangelist

Here is another one of the five ministry offices that has reasonably wide acceptance but not many direct mentions in scripture. Outside of Ephesians 4, the only two other places the word *evangelist* is used are in Acts 21:8, speaking of Philip, and in 2 Timothy 4:5, where Paul told his spiritual son to "*do the work of an evangelist.*"

So we see right away that the evangelist has specific "work" attached to his ministry, and since Philip is the only person directly named an evangelist, his ministry must be a showcase, of sorts, of the evangelistic ministry.

We first hear of Philip when he was selected to be a deacon (Acts 6:5). So we can see that not only was he an active member of the local congregation, he was among those who had a good reputation and was full of the Holy Spirit and wisdom.

Being faithful in a local church, serving with humility, and having a good reputation is the starting point for all the ministries we see in the New Testament. None of those with New Testament ministries were rogue individuals who just decided to start their own ministerial enterprise! This lets us know the quality of individuals the early Church looked for. Undoubtedly this was one of the reasons why the early Church was successful in stewarding the anointing to both gather and govern the house of God and affect the regions.

> *Then Philip went down to the city of Samaria and preached Christ to them. And the multitudes with one accord heeded the things spoken by Philip, hearing and seeing the miracles which he did. For unclean spirits, crying with a loud voice, came out of many who were possessed; and many who were paralyzed and lame were healed. And there was great joy in that city (Acts 8:5–8).*

From his humble beginnings as a deacon in Acts 6, we now see Philip preaching with signs and wonders following in Acts 8. A lot can happen to a faithful man in two chapters!

Philip the deacon became Philip the evangelist, the only person named as such in scripture. What little the Holy Spirit saw fit to let us know about Philip's ministry in these few verses says a lot about what an evangelist is and does.

Philip preached Christ. This sums up the office of an evangelist! Evangelists are not motivational speakers who preach a feel-good message to coerce people to join a church. Jesus said, *"And I, if I am lifted up from the earth, will draw all peoples to Myself"* (John 12:32). This is the principle by which the ministry of an evangelist operates—they lift Christ up before man. Then Jesus Himself, through the power of the Spirit, draws men to Himself. The anointing is released as the Gospel is preached.

Paul said it this way in Romans 1:16, *"For I am not ashamed of the gospel of Christ, for it is the power of God to salvation for everyone who believes, for the Jew first and also for the Greek."* Years ago, as a very young minister, I made a few trips to India to participate on the crusade team with a seasoned crusade evangelist. He would preach on an open field to thousands every night and have all sorts of healing miracles happen as he ministered. Many demon-possessed people would dance and writhe their way down toward the altar area as he was preaching. I noticed that he never stopped to minister to them or to cast demons out of them. He would simply go on preaching a very simple, basic Gospel message, and invariably by the end of the meeting, I would see those same people who had been writhing under demonic torment be completely set free. It was a demonstration of what power is inherent in the Gospel! In a crusade that size, with that many demon-possessed in manifestation, had he stopped preaching to minister to each one individually, he would have lost the crowd. So in that situation, he continued lifting Christ up, and the power of God was released in the preaching of Christ!

The supernatural is inevitably available whenever the Gospel is presented. The office of the evangelist, as found in Ephesians 4, is a trumpet that proclaims Christ as Savior. It is part of the gathering and governing anointing.

The supernatural is inevitably available whenever the Gospel is presented.

Because the church I was involved in after I got born again as a young teenager was Spirit filled with a great love for missions and evangelism, I was exposed to many evangelists who preached there regularly. They all had great healing and miracles accompanying their preaching. I thought all evangelists *had to* have healing miracles accompanying their preaching until I later discovered that there were others who had very effectively filled stadiums and have the altars full each time but did not seem to have the same emphasis on healing and miracles that Spirit-filled congregations do.

I wondered about this for quite a while until I saw that first, besides the office of the evangelist, there is also a ministry of exhortation (Romans 12:8). The ministry of exhortation is one that exhorts or encourages people to get saved. There are not necessarily signs and wonders attached to it. Second, the office of evangelist is a function of Jesus' ministry as listed in Ephesians 4, part of the anointing to gather and govern. The working of miracles, gifts of healings, and others are a function of the Spirit's ministry as listed in 1 Corinthians 2, part of the anointing to go. It is always possible with God to partake of one aspect of His provision without allowing for certain other aspects. Clearly, it is possible to preach a message of salvation without preaching healing and deliverance just as it is possible to receive Jesus as Savior but not as Provider.

As soon as I saw this, I told the Lord that as far as I was concerned, I wanted help so that my heart would always be set on "yes and amen" to all the promises of God I saw in the Word (2 Corinthians 1:20)! I want salvation, healing, deliverance, and all else that He promised me!

Looking at what the Word lets us know of Philip, the New Testament's only clearly identified evangelist, we can readily see that signs and wonders, healings and deliverances were definitely part of the evangelist's ministry. The Mark 16 record of the Great Commission supports this model of evangelism—the preaching of the Word is accompanied by the demonstrations of the Spirit.

Even though Philip was used by the Lord to spark a revival in Samaria, the ministry that the Lord wanted for the Samaritans wasn't complete until the arrival of Peter and John from Jerusalem. Even though Philip got the Samaritans saved, healed, and delivered, typical of an evangelist, he seemingly did not go on to teach them the fundamental new-creation truths of the realities of being born again in Christ, including being filled with the Holy Spirit. It took the apostolic ministries of Peter and John to do that. This vividly demonstrates what we have looked at—the ministry gifts rely on each other, one planting, another watering, and God bringing the increase.

You could say that Philip gathered the Samaritans and Peter and John brought the governance of God to them!

CHAPTER 11

THE FOUNDATION OF THE APOSTLES AND PROPHETS

Having been built on the foundation of the apostles and prophets, Jesus Christ Himself being the chief cornerstone

(Ephesians 2:20).

There are two ways that this verse can be interpreted and I believe both are correct.

The first is that the apostles and prophets are the foundation on which the Church is built. Because the Bible was primarily recorded by prophets in the Old Testament and by apostles in the New Testament, and since the Word is our foundation, we can rightly say we are built on the foundation of the recorded ministry of the apostle and the prophet.

The second is that the ongoing active ministries of apostles and prophets today stabilizes and nourishes the Church by bringing forth fresh revelation. Apostles and prophets today do not receive or give new revelation, since the cannon of scripture is firmly complete, but they remind their generation of what God has already said and done and in doing so bring into the "now" what God said and did in the "then"!

The anointing that gathers and governs is a mantle of leadership. True godly leadership functions under the leadership of God. From a position of submission to God is where He intends that earthly leaders get their authority. There is divine order to the flow of authority, to the flow of the anointing.

These five ministry gifts are offices that God has called and anointed to facilitate the gathering of the Church and then to provide immediate, on the ground, day-to-day leadership. This is the context when we say that there is an anointing to govern: first, that the leadership of a local church is most commonly the pastor, someone who is called to ministry and to that local body; second, that the leadership of the Body of Christ at large, in safeguarding doctrinal soundness and providing Spirit-led strategic oversight, lies with those who are from within the five-fold ministry.

Scripturally and practically, it is not a requirement that local churches have all five ministry offices as part of their working staff. A local church should have covenant relationships with other ministry gifts besides their pastor, but it is not a scriptural requirement for every church to have an apostle as the senior pastor, a prophet as an associate pastor, an evangelist as the outreach pastor, a pastor as the visitation minister, and a teacher in charge of Sunday school! I have seen churches where they did have those five offices attending and working among them, but that was always something that organically happened and not just because the church felt a need to appoint people whom they thought walked in those offices or, worse, give people those titles just because they thought they needed to have that as part of church hierarchy.

Outside of the pastor, the other four of the ministry offices generally have traveling ministries so it would not be tenable to have them on staff to look after the daily affairs of the local church anyway. There are pastors who are also apostles or prophets or evangelists or teachers, but every pastor does not additionally need to be any one of those others in order to lead a local church. It is good that local churches have relationships with and hear from the other ministry gifts. That is part of divine order and ensures that the local congregation has access to all the flows of the anointing.

The anointing flows in fullness through divine order. Perhaps that is why the ministry offices of the apostle and the prophet have been fought against so hard by the enemy, either in getting the Church to deny their ongoing relevance or to puff them up to a place of scripturally unrealistic importance. All the ministry offices have an interdependence on each other, but this is especially true of the apostolic and prophetic ministry offices.

As I had earlier said, an often-used and accurate way to describe and remember the five-fold ministries would be to visualize an open hand. The little finger, sometimes called the pinkie finger, reminds us of the teacher. It is the slimmest and shortest finger, and so is the most abled to get to the smallest openings in the body, reaching the inner parts of the ear and nose to clean them. The teacher is able to deposit the Word in our "inner ears"!

The ring finger represents the pastor because, like the ring finger, he is in love with and married to the sheep. The wedding ring is worn on this finger because it symbolizes a heart connection, and that is what pastors have with the sheep.

The longest finger is the middle finger and that reminds us of the evangelist because he will go the longest distance to preach Christ.

Next is the pointing finger. This speaks of the prophet because the prophet points the way the Church needs to go and points at the things we need to fix!

Then last, the thumb represents the apostle because—as the apostle can prophesy, evangelize, pastor, and teach—it is the only finger that can easily touch all the other fingers.

Prophets see and say. Apostles hear and do. And both are needed to lay the foundations of what God intends for every generation.

The Prophet

Prophets speak from an inspiration, an impulse, that comes upon them from a sudden bubbling of revelation. What they do utter, in that moment, is the mind of the Spirit for moments past, present, or regarding a future event.

When prophesying, they speak from direct divine inspiration, not something they had preplanned.

Like the other ministry gifts, prophets are first and foremost ministers of the Gospel, preachers, or teachers of the Word. All believers may prophesy; some will progress, being more prophetic than others, and then there are others who will be called to the office of prophet.

Philip's four daughters *"did prophesy"* (Acts 21:8), meaning that they operated in the basic gift of prophecy, speaking edification, exhortation, and comfort (1 Corinthians 14:3).

Then verse 10 says that there was a *"certain prophet named Agabus."* He did not just prophesy but stood in the office of prophet.

To stand in the office of a prophet is evidenced by the regularity of the manifestations of the revelation gifts of the Spirit (word of wisdom, word of knowledge, or the discerning of spirits) and the gift of prophecy. The nine gifts of the Spirit listed in 1 Corinthians 12 are what empowers the believer and qualifies the minister.

Again, we see how all the anointings and giftings flow together toward the building of the Church.

Every believer has access to the gifts of the Spirit, but only those called to be a prophet will have these manifestations of revelation on a consistent, stronger flow. The prophet has an ongoing ministry along these lines, whereas a believer can have manifestations along these lines.

When the prophet ministers, there is a depth of the anointing that can be sensed that is beyond when a believer operates in the revelation gifts of the Spirit. The difference is the believer flows in the gifts while a prophet stands in the office. The gifts of the Spirit manifest as necessary through believers, but the five offices of Jesus reside in those called to that particular office. The former is a manifestation; the latter is a ministry.

Believers might have manifestations involving aspects of the prophetic while prophets have a ministry in the prophetic.

Another aspect of the anointing on the ministry of the prophet is that it illuminates his spiritual eyes so that he has visions and revelations.

The prophets were also called seers in the Old Testament because they would see and know things by the Spirit supernaturally.

There are three main types of visions.

Spiritual visions are when a person sees in his spirit.

Spiritual visions are when a person sees in his spirit. It is, in a sense, an inner vision. These are not just mental images from an over-active imagination but come up, many times unexpectedly, from deep within, from the Holy Spirit through the human spirit. Spiritual visions come with a sense of His Presence and a knowing that does not accompany mental vision. Paul's Damascus road experience in Acts 9:1-8 was a spiritual vision: *"when his eyes were opened, he saw no one"* (Acts 9:8) tells us that Paul was not seeing with his natural eyes but with his spiritual eyes. Spiritual visions are seen with spiritual eyes.

Trances are the second type of vision. In a trance, the physical senses are suspended and contact with the physical realm is seemingly absent. A trance is not when a person is unconscious but simply that they are more conscious of the spiritual realm than of the physical realm. Peter fell into a trance on the housetop as he was praying (Acts 10:10). The revelation he received while in that trance changed the trajectory of the Church because it was from that encounter that the early leadership finally understood that Jesus did not just mean the Israelites when He commanded them to "go into all the world." Trances can bring clarity to the instructions of the Word and the Spirit. Actually, all communications from the Spirit bring understanding and amplification to the things of God as already declared in the Word.

> *In a trance, the physical senses are suspended and contact with the physical realm is seemingly absent.*

Bringing clarifying revelation is part of a prophet's ministry as teacher and preacher of the Word. *Prophets do not just foretell, predictively, they also tell forth the things of God!*

I have had people fall into trances during my services. In one particular service, the pastor's wife fell into a trance, standing with her hands lifted in worship. She stayed in that one spot, in that same position, for nearly an hour before she came back to an awareness of the natural realm.

The third type of vision is an open vision. Like a spiritual vision, this is when a person sees in the spirit realm, but unlike a trance, the physical senses are not suspended. So in an open vision, the senses of both realms are awakened and opened at once. This is what John experienced on the isle of Patmos when he received what we have today in the Bible as Revelation. John was aware of his physical location (Revelation 1:9) but was also aware of being *"in the Spirit on the Lord's Day, and I heard"* (Revelation 1:10). John was aware of physically being on Patmos but he was also hearing in the Spirit!

> *The third type of vision is an open vision. Like a spiritual vision, this is when a person sees in the spirit realm, but unlike a trance, the physical senses are not suspended. So in*

an open vision, the senses of both realms are awakened and opened at once.

This is true for all believers everywhere, but I have witnessed that it is especially true for those called to be prophets. Prophets need to maintain a strong grounding in the Word so that their devotional inner life is steady. This inner fortitude is necessary because the prophet's ministry is oftentimes dramatic. People are generally intrigued with the delivery of a prophetic utterance. And sometimes that intrigue can go unchecked and become a demand for the prophet to "perform" and deliver a word regardless of the leading of the Spirit. It takes character and a fear of God to say no in those situations. Attempting to move in the Spirit in general and the prophetic in particular without knowing or being led by the Spirit of God opens the door up for familiar spirits to operate.

Balaam in Numbers 22 was such an example. Saul seeking out the witch of En Dor in 1 Samuel 28 is another. A word from the Lord cannot be forced, but it is considerably easier to get a word from any other spirit! So those called to the office of a prophet and those who move in the prophetic must have strength enough to move with the Spirit when He moves and strength enough not to move when the Spirit isn't moving.

Prophets should be free to know that they will not know everything about everyone every time! This frees them from the pressure of performing.

Gehazi, Elisha's servant, evidently knew this because even though he was around the prophet all the time, he dared to attempt lying to Elisha. If Gehazi had known Elisha to know of everything at all times, he wouldn't have dared try (2 Kings 5:20-27). Of course, Gehazi did get exposed by Elisha, but Gehazi was willing to risk it because he knew his master did not always know everything.

A prophet is supposed to do more than just prophesy. They are full-fledged ministers of the Gospel. This is why prophets must maintain a strong Word life, like any other believer. *Prophets should minister the written Word if the Spirit is not in manifestation for the revealed Word.* Forcing or, worse, faking a prophetic word harms the Church and demeans the office of prophet.

Prefacing every statement with "the Lord told me" doesn't make one spiritual; it makes one suspect! God does speak, but He does not have to tell us everything!

It is the height of unholiness to claim the Holy Spirit said something when He did not!

This is a real way that I have seen believers train themselves to cooperate with unholy, familiar spirits.

> *Prefacing every statement with "the Lord told me" doesn't make one spiritual; it makes one suspect! It is the height of unholiness to claim the Holy Spirit said something when He did not!*

Since prophets are half of the foundation-laying duo, it is imperative that there be a purity to the prophetic that we have access to. To have a flow of putrid prophetic would hurt the foundations of the Church!

Healing is often an accompaniment to the prophet's ministry. Actually, anytime the Word of the Lord is proclaimed there is a portal for healing opened. This is especially so with the prophet's ministry because they deliver a "now" word from the Lord.

As one of the five ministry anointings, the prophet stands at the forefront of leadership within the Body. This means the prophet is among those who are to lead the Church toward maturity and ministry. *It takes maturity to lead the Church to maturity.* I believe there is a whole company of tried, tested, and true prophets reserved and preserved for this generation!

The Apostle

As only the thumb on the hand can touch all the other fingers, so the apostle has a unique role in the Body. Apostles pioneer, plant, and produce. They pioneer a message that God entrusts to them. They then plant a work that those who have received that message can gather around. The work they plant will ultimately reproduce that message in and then through the lives of those who have gathered.

Leaders are many times raised up by the apostles to continue the work that they planted, which then frees the apostle so that they can move on to plant more works. The founding apostle usually continues having a relationship with the works they plant after they have handed day-to-day leadership over.

Apostles tend to employ a fathering model of leadership over a managerial model. This is because an apostle's heart for ministry, second only to their heart for God, is to give birth to the things of God on the earth. The apostle's ability, by the anointing, to gather and govern is due to the apostle's fathering nature in ministry. Pastors may be a spiritual father to their congregation, but apostles tend to be spiritual fathers to ministers and ministries as opposed to individuals.

There are different degrees or categories of each of the five ministry offices.

Of course, at the head of each category of office is Jesus Himself. This is to say that for each of the five ministry offices, Jesus alone functioned in the fullness of the measure of the anointing allotted to that office. He operated in full what all others called to that office have only in measure. So Jesus is the top category of apostle (Hebrews 3:1).

The second category of apostles are the original twelve apostles of the Lamb. This includes Matthias, who replaced Judas. In a very real way, these twelve apostles are part of the foundation of the Church Ephesians 2 talks about (Revelation 21:14). They are unique because they were actual companions and witnesses to the earthly ministry of Jesus (Acts 1:15-22).

The third category of apostles is the category that Paul was in. These are the other New Testament foundational apostles. Although Paul was not an eyewitness companion to Jesus, he was called and anointed to scribe a major part of the New Testament we have. In doing so, Paul had revelation of things that the original twelve apostles did not and laid a foundation that they could not have, which we still build on today.

The last and largest grouping of apostles are those who arose after the New Testament books had been written. This extends to our present-day apostles. They are not foundational apostles in the sense that the initial apostles became. They write or lay no New Testament writings or doctrines, but they are equipped to expound and build upon the foundations already laid. In that sense, they did not light the flame, but they are keepers of the flame.

With this understanding, it is easy to see why the apostle is well equipped with the anointing to govern the Church in the things of the Spirit.

It is not scriptural or necessary to have an apostle "rule" or govern a local church. The New Testament foundational apostles did not seek or maintain positional leadership over churches they started. They did, however, have spiritual oversight. The practical oversight was delegated to others once the apostles left the churches they had established (Acts 20:28).

Apostolic oversight, from their fathering heart, is based on relationship, not ecclesiastical hierarchy.

I was ministering once at a church and was led to start talking about apostolic authority and the role of apostles in the local church. I mentioned that I had known of people who were going around to churches they had no relationship with, handing out calling cards to announce themselves as apostles and then offer to be the church's apostle and the pastor's spiritual father. And all they wanted in return for that honor was a portion of church's regular tithe and offering! A man who was seated near the back, by the exit, got up and left abruptly. I didn't think anything of it until later one of the pastors there told me that that man had been making the rounds to local churches, offering to be their apostle for a monthly subscription fee! If anything, that is apostolic disorder, not apostolic order!

In this aspect, we need to be like the church in Ephesus that Jesus through John wrote to in Revelation 2—we need to judge those who call themselves apostles to see if they indeed are (Revelation 2:2).

If the Ephesian church could mark out false apostles, there must then also be marks of true apostles.

True apostolic ministry is marked by humility. The works and fruit of an apostle are revealed before there are public proclamations of their office! Apostles are purposeful because apostles are literally "sent ones" and you cannot be sent by God without a purpose.

- *True apostles will have a heart for the welfare of the whole Body of Christ.* They may not get to the whole Body to minister to them, but their heart will be for the whole Body. Their mission will be the edifying of the Body of Christ, taking Ephesians 4:11–16 to heart.
- *True apostles will not have a covetous spirit.* This was part of how Judas disqualified himself from apostleship. This is true for every one of the ministry offices but especially so for the apostle. Apostles have to be faithful stewards before and after the multitudes sell their possessions and lay them at their feet (Acts 4:34–37)!

- *True apostles are not people pleasers nor do they care to be.* Their mannerism, because of the determination and drive they have, many times seems to go against the culture of the day. They are examples of what "tough love" can look like!

- *True apostles have a supernatural ministry* both in deed and in word. Just as they can touch all the other functions of the other four ministry offices, they have an ease flowing in the nine gifts of the Spirit listed in 1 Corinthians 12. There is no other way that the apostle can get his mission accomplished. Apostles have supernatural manifestations accompanying their revelatory teaching and preaching.

- *True apostles minister divine discipline and correction supernaturally.* Whenever the Church is at a crossroads doctrinally, ethically or morally, apostles have the divine grace to administer a course correction. They keep the Church pure from within and without.

- *True apostles think regionally and globally.* They love the local church but see beyond the local church. Many times they see the local church as a vehicle through which the region can be brought under the influence of God. They take the Great Commission personally and strategically.

- *True apostles associate with and are recognized by other five-fold ministers.* Paul associated with Barnabas and was recognized by the leadership in Jerusalem. Jesus was recognized by John the Baptist. Timothy was discipled and recognized by Paul. We have no example in the New Testament of "lone wolf" ministers—individuals who were not in association with other ministers but were off on their own, running their own ministry. Such an individual places himself outside of the corporate anointing and cuts himself off from the rest of the Body—exactly the position the enemy would like them in!

A Little Bit More About Governing

All the five ministry gifts are sent by God to nourish and mature the Church. A basic New Testament truth is the priesthood of every believer (1 Peter 2:9). No believer is dependent on anyone else to communicate with God. This does not mean that believers are to be independent of the Body but that God has created us to be interdependent on other members in the Body. The ministry gifts are not meant to be a go-between or a mediator of sorts between God and the believer.

Neither are the ministry gifts as listed in Ephesians 4 meant to be a recipe for church structure.

> *And God has appointed these in the church: first apostles, second prophets, third teachers, after that miracles, then gifts of healings, helps, administrations, varieties of tongues* (1 Corinthians 12:28).

The King James Version uses the word *governments* instead of *administrations*, and the New Living Translation says *leadership*.

God placed this gift of governance, administration, or leadership in the Body because He is the God of order, not confusion. Having governance listed separately from the other gifts immediately tells us that governing itself is not inherent in the other offices.

The fact is that, scripturally, the New Testament speaks of the need to have governance in the church but does not lay out a detailed plan of universal governance for the Church. I believe that this is on purpose because the Holy Spirit knew that in the 2,000 or so years to follow, what the Church would face would greatly change. Revelation on principles to govern the Church was clearly spelled out but not a definite method of organization.

This book is not a study on church structure, nor is it a full study on the apostles' and prophets' office. It is a study on how the anointing manifests in different but all-encompassing ways so that the Church can grow, go, and be gathered and governed by the plans and ways of God.

I have seen too many, too often assume the title of *prophet* or *apostle* to bolster themselves into a position of leadership. While it is definitely true that apostles and prophets are leaders, that is always only the case if the person called to that office answers the call in humility, obedience, and a heart attitude of discipleship.

It hurts the Body of Christ when we blindly accept those who do not practically meet the scriptural standards of apostleship or, really, any of the other ministry offices. When we accept the imitations as the genuine, we immediately loose our ability to seek after and receive from the genuine.

I believe that the Church's best days are yet ahead of us. And this means that all aspects of the anointing will be in fuller availability and manifestation. It is not too soon for believers everywhere to be trained to flow in the ways of the anointing! We must be willing to forsake the enticing but temporary entrapments of a "glamorous" Church and push toward being the *glorious Church!*

CHAPTER 12

THE GREATER ANOINTING

The anointing to gather leads the way to another aspect of the anointing—the corporate anointing. The greatest possible flow of the anointing is found in the corporate flow. I am well convinced that if we got the Body of Christ together as a single unit, we would have the same measure of the Spirit as Jesus did. *Individually, we are part of the Body; collectively, we **are** the Body!*

When the Temple of God was dedicated in 2 Chronicles 5, we see that the whole building was filled with the glory cloud (2 Chronicles 5:11-14). This is actually a pattern we see throughout the Old Testament—the glory cloud would fill the house of God. Everything that we see in the Old Testament is a type and shadow of Christ and the Church (Colossians 2:17). In the New Testament, we see that we, the Body of Christ, are also called the Temple and house of God (1 Corinthians 3:16). *The man-built temple in the Old Testament is a picture of the Spirit-built Temple in the New Testament.* If the glory cloud filled the man-made temple, how much more must God want to fill the Spirit-built Temple of the Body of Christ! This is why the enemy encourages isolation and division. *The more he can get us to scatter, the less of the glory we can contain.*

One thing that the temple in the Old Testament facilitated was corporate worship. Something powerful is released when the people of God come together to worship God. Worship focuses us on Him, lifting and honoring Him high above all else. True worship extols His virtues. True worship reminds us of all He is and not just what we seek. God is seeking those who will worship Him in Spirit and in truth (John 4:23-24).

My heart has been grieved as I noticed that the trend in many circles today is to sing contemporarily, upbeat songs that have a rhythmic, catchy beat that is emotionally stirring but is very light on honoring and recognizing Him and what has been accomplished for us by Jesus. A lot of what we call contemporary worship songs are really pop or love songs with Christian verbiage thrown in. They were recorded to be playlist friendly instead of Presence friendly. They evoke our emotions but not our hearts toward God. Such songs have a beat but do not make room for the Presence. It is clear that many of these songs were conceived in any room other than the Throne Room!

Sadly, it seems we have substituted natural abilities for the anointing when it comes to who leads us in worship. Of course, I believe that those leading us in worship should have musical abilities. Songs, even spiritual songs, will affect our emotions but the difference is that soulish songs *only* affect us emotionally. Soulish songs do not draw us closer to Him, do not lift Him up, do not honor the already complete work of Jesus, and make no room for the Spirit to move. I am also aware and agree that every generation will have their own sound and beat, so I am not against contemporary songs in church. But *we cannot afford to swap "contemporary" for heavenly!* I believe we can have contemporary songs that come to us from heaven and usher us into the Presence of God!

Many of what we call "classic" worship songs and hymns—like John Newton's "Amazing Grace" (1779), Fanny Crosby's "Blessed Assurance" (1873), and Pastor Jack Hayford's "Majesty" (2004), which carry such a weight of the glory when we sing them—were once considered contemporary songs! John and Charles Wesley, brothers who founded the Methodist church (1784), firebrands for the things of God in their day, wrote over 6,500 hymns! They wrote theology, zeal, fervor, and worship *into* their music!

Most of the places I minister in do not sing hymns. And that is fine. I hardly sing hymns myself. My point is when you look at the history of worship and music in the Church, you very quickly see that the songs they sang were not just for feel-good entertainment, but to honor God and usher His Presence into their midst! Further back, in the Old Testament, the psalms were the hymnal of their day, and we can safely say that none of those were sung for their entertainment!

Just as every generation must have their own revelation of Jesus, every generation must be free to worship Him in their own vernacular. We must make room for modern-day worship songs—as long as they actually are songs that worship and not just emotions set to music!

We have gotten so used to having smoke machines during our worship services that we have forgotten to make room for the glory cloud!

A young worship leader asked me one day over lunch what I'd like to see more of from worship leaders. Right away, I told him that first I would like to have more worship and fewer concert performances, and second, I would like to see more leadership, meaning I would like for the worship leader to lead the congregation to His Presence and not try to entertain us or just sing to us as they play through their "set"!

Worship becomes a powerful weapon for the Church when it is an acceptable offering to God!

Corporate Gatherings and Corporate Prayer

Another way we get to a greater anointing is through corporate prayer.

Corporate prayer, in essence, is not when we meet to pray for our needs. Corporate prayer is when we gather to seek God and ask Him to speak to us. In corporate prayer, we collectively come as one to fall on our faces before God. *It is in corporate prayer that the Church extends the government of God on the earth.*

> *Now in the church that was at Antioch there were certain prophets and teachers: Barnabas, Simeon who was called Niger, Lucius of Cyrene, Manaen who had been brought up with Herod the tetrarch, and Saul. As they ministered to the Lord and fasted, the Holy Spirit said, "Now separate to Me Barnabas and Saul for the work to which I have called them." Then, having fasted and prayed, and laid hands on them, they sent them away* (Acts 13:1-3).

This prayer meeting with five men drew forth a word from the Lord. They were not meeting to ask anything of God. All they did was to minister to Him. This means they magnified Him. This could have been in speaking or singing words of adoration and lifting up the name and personhood of God. Whenever I have pondered what it was that these five men did in ministering to God, I have always had the sense that it was akin to how the four living creatures and the twenty-four elders worshiped God around His throne room in Revelation 4.

> *The four living creatures, each having six wings, were full of eyes around and within. And they do not rest day or night, saying: "Holy, holy, holy, Lord God Almighty, who was and is and is to come!"*
>
> *Whenever the living creatures give glory and honor and thanks to Him who sits on the throne, who lives forever and ever, the twenty-four elders fall down before Him who sits on the throne and worship*

Him who lives forever and ever, and cast their crowns before the throne, saying:

You are worthy, O Lord, to receive glory and honor and power; for You created all things, and by Your will they exist and were created (Revelation 4:8-11).

To magnify God is to purposely place Him high above all else by our words, thoughts, and actions. Anywhere in the Bible that you see the worship of God encouraged or instructed, it always involves declaring how high and lifted up God is. The focus is strictly on God and not on man. And in magnifying God, He always responds with His Presence.

And of course, as Paul himself instructed the Ephesians to pray with all manner of praying (Ephesians 6:18), they must have prayed in the Spirit, in tongues. We know that for Paul, praying in tongues was a major part of his prayer life (1 Corinthians 14:18).

In response to the arrest of Peter and John, we see in Acts 4:24:

So when they heard that, they raised their voice to God with one accord and said: "Lord, You are God, who made heaven and earth and the sea, and all that is in them."

Notice it doesn't say "they raised their *voices*" but that they raised their *voice*, singular. This is what a Spirit-led corporate prayer meeting sounds like—many voices yielding to the Spirit and becoming one voice. Such unity is only possible in the Spirit, by the Spirit.

This one voice was not just that those praying were united with each other but that in the Spirit they were united with Him.

Let the word of Christ dwell in you richly in all wisdom, teaching and admonishing one another in psalms and hymns and spiritual songs, singing with grace in your hearts to the Lord (Colossians 3:16).

This verse is a sampling of what should happen when believers gather with "one another." But Paul then goes on to admonish us to sing with grace in our hearts *to the Lord*. So evidently, not only can we minister to one another but we can also minister to the Lord!

There is much power available when one believer gives in to prayer led by the Spirit. But when there is a corporate gathering and a room full of believers who give in to the Spirit together, that is when the plans of God are birthed on the earth and regions are bought into alignment with the plans of God. *We don't just need more prayer in the Church. We need more Spirit-led prayer in the Church!*

Part of the anointing's function to gather and govern the Body is that while we are seated in heavenly places in Christ here on earth, a singular, unified voice can roar across the physical landscape to usher in Kingdom rule on earth as in heaven!

It takes the anointing to gather the Body of Christ so that the anointing of divine governance can be enacted across the land!

It takes corporate prayer to birth the things of the Spirit, and it takes the anointing to birth corporate prayer!

Pray by the Anointing; Pray into the Anointing

Corporate prayer is not the only form of prayer that taps into the anointing. Actually, corporate prayer is strengthened by individual prayer. *A call to corporate prayer is a gathering and a governing of the Body so that the Body can gather the harvest and govern in the Spirit realm!*

In developing our individual prayer life, we open ourselves up to the spirit realm. This is why Spirit-led praying, praying at the prompting and the unction of the Spirit, and praying in tongues are vital to developing sensitivity to the anointing.

Just as in the natural some churches and prayer groups have set times to meet and pray about certain things, the Spirit also has times that He wants certain things prayed about. I have always said that there should be no contest if I had to choose between my prayer list and the Holy Spirit's prayer list! It is the carnal mind that imagines that our prayer needs are all that need to be prayed about without realizing that the Holy Spirit also wants things prayed out on the earth so that the plans of God can be birthed and manifested in this realm. *To pray as led by the Spirit is a powerful aspect of partnership with God.* Another benefit of praying as led by the Spirit is that we learn to follow the promptings of the Spirit. It takes a sensitivity to the Spirit to know when and what He wants us praying about. *In yielding to the Spirit through prayer, we learn both His voice and His ways!*

Praying is not always and only praying in tongues; rather, it is praying from the position of the Spirit—in any language! However, praying in tongues is a primary way that we tune our spirits to the Holy Spirit's frequency. And more often than not, praying in the Spirit will involve praying in tongues. In the natural, we only speak the languages we do because of our natural upbringing and surroundings. Conversely, when we are more aware of the spirit realm than we are of the natural realm, it's only natural that we speak in a supernatural tongue, which is the language of the spirit realm! Tongues shift our attention and focus off our natural surroundings. This does not mean that a believer has to be in an ecstatic state to speak in tongues. Paul said, "*I will pray with the spirit, and I will also pray with the understanding. I will sing with the spirit, and I will also sing with the understanding*" (1 Corinthians 14:15). Evidently, Paul understood that he could *will* to pray and sing in the spirit just as he could *will* to pray and sing in the natural, with his understanding. The context of this verse in 1 Corinthians is speaking in tongues.

Like Paul, the more we will our natural tongues to the tongues of the spirit, the more the tongues of the spirit becomes natural to us!

Praying and speaking in tongues acquaints and orients us to the spiritual realm, which is where the anointing originates. I often see tongues as the highway that transports the natural to the spirit realm and the spiritual to the natural realm!

It is no coincidence that Paul, who boldly declared that he spoke in tongues more than the believers at Corinth (1 Corinthians 14:18), was also responsible for yielding to the Spirit in scribing the bulk of the New Testament and receiving the mysteries of the new birth!

We are, today, still recipients of Paul's prayer and discoveries in the spirit.

Like Paul, we too need to value and purposely *will* to venture into the spirit by praying in tongues. The more we yield our tongue to the Spirit, the more the Spirit can say to and through us! And the Spirit speaking is the fount from which the anointing flows!

Anointed for Regions

The corporate worship and prayer meetings that the early Church held functioned as spiritual birthing rooms and launching pads for the initial apostles and the early Church. Despite their call to go into all the world, they had neither the insight or "want to" to do so. *The anointing only accompanies the call as it is answered.* The anointing lies latent until the call is acted on. The apostles, literally meaning "sent ones," were technically not functioning as apostles until they agreed with Jesus sending them and went. But the moment they did, as they obeyed Jesus' command, all through the book of Acts the anointing met them and manifested through them!

The calling of God is in relation to regions and people groups. This is why God sent Paul to the Gentile world (Romans 11:13) and Peter to the Jewish world (Galatians 2:8). God was sending workmen to His fields—His regions! We can say that for every people group and region, God has called ones so that they can go and be sent ones! This demonstrates both the anticipative and compassionate nature of God. Anticipative, in His foreknowing, knows that there will be those who need to hear and will respond if offered an opportunity. Compassionate, because God sends laborers, like Jonah to Nineveh, many times not because people want or even deserve to hear but because of God's love. *Callings from God to regions are because of His mercy toward people groups, and the anointing to go in to that region is that mercy in action!*

Apostles many times will have a specific region that they are sent to or a message that they are sent with.

> *So pray to the Lord who is in charge of the harvest; ask him to send more workers into his fields* (Matthew 9:38 NLT).

As I was studying this one time, the Lord said to me, "I send laborers into the fields, not just to stalks of wheat." Thank God for the ones won to Christ individually, but God intends for a net-breaking catch of fish and not just those we can get on a fishing rod! The laborers are sent to "fields"—this includes individuals, but the plan and will of God is the entire plot of land! It takes one anointing to go to individuals and another anointing to go to regions!

The anointing to gather and govern mobilizes the Body of Christ so that we can stay in step with the Spirit and walk into all the regions that are ready to be harvested!

That God called Paul, educated in the Law and the intricacies of the Jewish world, to the Gentiles and Peter, an entrepreneur, a working fisherman to the Jewish community showed that God does not choose or send anyone based on natural ability or social preparedness alone. God expects a dependance on the anointing from those He calls and sends. If it were up to a missions board's vote, they would have sent Paul to the Jews and Peter to the Gentiles!

Faithfulness to the call of God and the accompanying anointing is what qualifies anyone!

Staying in the Greater Flow

And do not be drunk with wine, in which is dissipation; but be filled with the Spirit, speaking to one another in psalms and hymns and spiritual songs, singing and making melody in your heart to the Lord, giving thanks always for all things to God the Father in the name of our Lord Jesus Christ, submitting to one another in the fear of God (Ephesians 5:18–21).

This is not just a passage about our individual spiritual practices but there is a corporate element about it. Paul here tells us to speak "to one another." So that implies a corporate gathering. *When believers gather, the possibility of having a wider variety of spiritual manifestations is multiplied.* When we congregate, the individual spark of the Spirit on each one of us is fanned into a combustion of explosive, divine power!

The right associations in our lives through God-ordained relationships will enhance and enrich the anointing in and on our lives. As we have seen, the anointing is an invisible yet tangible heavenly substance, and because it is tangible, it is also transmittable and transferable. In a corporate setting, not only is the depth of the anointing on us individually stirred and pulled out of us by the depth of the anointing in the room, but the anointing on the other believers, as it overflows from them, spills and splashes onto us!

After that you shall come to the hill of God where the Philistine garrison is. And it will happen, when you have come there to the

178

city, that you will meet a group of prophets coming down from the high place with a stringed instrument, a tambourine, a flute, and a harp before them; and they will be prophesying. Then the Spirit of the Lord will come upon you, and you will prophesy with them and be turned into another man (1 Samuel 10:5-6).

If this could be so under the Old Covenant, as we see here with Saul, how much more can the corporate anointing affect us under the New Covenant! The associations we keep and the rooms we gather in affect us in more ways than believers have understood.

The anointings that we gather under, that disciple us, also shape us through impartations. So if we sit under an anointed teacher, they will invariably leave a residue of that teaching anointing in and on us. Of course, while we need all the five ministry office anointings to nourish us, there will be certain ones that we will be led to maintain a discipling, mentoring relationship with. Such divinely led associations influence our thoughts and imprint our spirits. Personally, there have been numerous occasions when, as I was ministering, I have sensed and stepped into anointings that were on other ministers who had an influence on my life. I had not knowingly planned to speak like or mimic them in any way and I never will, but impartations have a way of bubbling up! The reverse is also true—if we continually allow for voices of doubt and chaos around us, that same thought process and spiritual function will have an influence over us. In desiring to develop a sensitivity to the anointing, who we allow to gather us matters!

Discipleship Is the Result of Gathering and Governing

The end result of the anointing to gather and govern us is really that we can be made disciples of Jesus! *It takes an anointing to be a disciple of the Anointed One!* Being a disciple is ultimately what God intends for every person who calls on the name of Jesus. Yielding to the anointing to gather and govern us is how we move from convert to disciple! *Converts are those who have believed in Jesus. Disciples are those who live the life of Jesus!*

Disciples are made by modeling after others. This happens when we hear about and then live out what is recorded for us in scripture, and it also happens when we imitate mature ministers as they imitate Christ (1 Corinthians 11:1). I have seen that many times God yokes believers to ministers who are more developed in the same calls and anointings that they themselves are called to, so that by precept and example those believers can learn about and see modeled what walking out their call and anointing looks like. Being a disciple is not meant to be a solitary pursuit. For sure, there are times when we as believers need to get alone to still our heart to commune with God, but it is important to remember that it is collectively that we are Jesus' Body! Jesus' command for us to make disciples emphasizes that God does not intend that we be believers alone. To make disciples requires at least two parties—the one making the disciple and the one being made a disciple! So there is a definite element of a necessary exchange, a transference, from one believer to another in discipleship. Of course, a disciple is not just one who is taught in the Word of the Lord but also one who is taught the ways of the Spirit. *It takes both the Word and the Spirit to make a disciple.*

The anointing does teach us personally and privately, but the anointing also teaches us corporately and publicly!

Flowing with the Flow

The anointing is vital to each and every aspect of the life of the believer and the vitality of the Church.

This study, while not intended to be a comprehensive look at the anointing, highlights the functions of the anointing through each of the main stages in the life of a believer.

After the sacrifice of Jesus, I see the anointing as the furtherance of the grace of God to us. In grace and mercy, Jesus died for us, and in grace and mercy the anointing is made available to us.

The sacrifice of Jesus offers us the life of God, and the outpouring of the Spirit empowers us to live the life of God!

The sacrifice of Jesus ushers us into the Presence of God, and the anointing seats us in heavenly places to rule and reign with Him!

The sacrifice of Jesus fills us with God's Presence, and the anointing of the Spirit is the outpouring of that life!

Both the sacrifice of Jesus and the outpouring of the Spirit in fire and oil from heaven are necessary so that God would have sons and daughters in the earth realm.

Just as the Word is ever living and continually speaks to us at any stage of our spiritual growth, so the anointing of the Spirit is ever present and able to manifest God in our everyday lives at every stage of our walk with God. In fact, the more mature we get in our walk with God, the more we will see the need for the Word and the Spirit in our lives, because it takes maturity to see that our dependence on God is continual as long as we walk with Him. The Word and the Spirit are so vast in breadth and depth that we will spend eternity plunging the depths of knowing all that God is and has for us!

There is much to be learned about the anointing, and it will take the anointing for it to be learned!

ABOUT JAMES TAN

Dr. James Tan is a visionary leader who declares the goodness of God and the reality of the Spirit to a new generation of believers. Sent forth to pioneer and establish a standard of the Word and the Spirit, he ministers scriptural insights while making room for the demonstrations of the Spirit. Ministering internationally, cross-culturally, and across denominational lines, James is a voice and mentor to a growing number of churches and ministries around the world.

From
KERRICK BUTLER

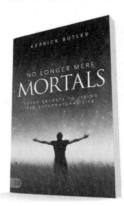

Real-Life Superheroes

YOU are Gods supernatural solution for a world beset with giant problems.

Pastor Kerrick Butler II encourages us that the problems we face in the world today must be addressed by a church who understands that we are not merely mortal, but supernaturally empowered by the Holy Spirit to conquer the Goliaths of our day.

In *No Longer Mere Mortals*, Kerrick shares how to

- Operate in Gods power as a lifestylenot a rare, momentary encounter
- Be empowered as a superhumannot just as an apostle, prophet, evangelist, pastor, or teacher
- Grow by leaps and bounds in daily Christian disciplines
- Understand who you are in Christ and what God has already accomplished in your life
- Unleash the supernatural powers God has already given you over specific issues

Defeat the Goliaths staring you down. You may not wear a cape, but God made you superhuman just the same!

Purchase your copy wherever books are sold

From
Alan DiDio

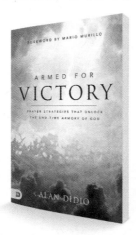

Are you struggling to overcome the spiritual enemies that are coming against you?
You may be using the wrong weaponry.

God is opening His armory and releasing weapons of warfare that haven't been seen in generations. The enemy is using these perilous end times to cause many believers to become worn out, depressed, and defeated because they are unwittingly using the wrong weapons in battle.

It's time to get equipped with the *right weapons*.

In *Armed for Victory,* pastor and author Alan DiDio brings revelation about spiritual warfare tactics that will empower and activate you for victory. Don't live one more day in deception, denial, or defeat. It's time to overcome!

You were born to win, and you have access to the intelligence, tools, and strategies that guarantee your victory. Learn these principles, use the right weapons, and secure victory in every battle!

Purchase your copy wherever books are sold.

From
James Tan

Shine Forth with a Flow of the Miraculous!

Why would a supernatural God build a supernatural Church and then expect it to function naturally? He wouldn't! God wants the gospel delivered and demonstrated by believers who live in a unique flow of the miraculous.

In *Releasing the Miraculous*, author and pastor James Tan shares that the Holy Spirit infilling is really about God outpouring Himself through operations we call the nine gifts of the Spirit.

In 1 Corinthians 12:7, the apostle Paul describes these gifts as manifestations of the Spirit, which in the Greek literally means a shining forth! That's God's plan for you—to shine forth with the light of God in the same way electricity manifests in countless ways around you every day.

No believer is "gift-less"! So yield yourself to the Spirit like never before because heaven is waiting on you to demonstrate the miraculous to the world!

Purchase your copy wherever books are sold.

In the Right Hands, This Book Will Change Lives!

Most of the people who need this message will not be looking for this book. To change their lives, you need to **put a copy of this book in their hands.**

Our ministry is constantly seeking methods to find the people who need this anointed message to change their lives. **Will you help us reach these people?**

Extend this ministry by sowing three, five, ten, or *even more* books today and change people's lives for the better! Your generosity will be part of catalyzing the Great Awakening that many have been prophesying and praying for.